CAKETOPIA

YOUR GUIDE TO DECORATING
BUTTERCREAM CAKES WITH FLAIR

SHERI WILSON
Founder of Cake Design by Sheri

PAGE STREET
PUBLISHING CO

PAGE STREET
PUBLISHING CO.

First published in 2021 by

Page Street Publishing Co.

27 Congress Street, Suite 105

Salem, MA 01970

www.pagestreetpublishing.com

Distributed by Macmillan, sales in Canada by The Canadian Manda Group.

25   24   23   22   21   1   2   3   4   5

ISBN-13: 978-1-64567-394-1

ISBN-10: 1-64567-394-4

Library of Congress Control Number: 2021931366

Cover and book design by Laura Benton for Page Street Publishing Co.

Photography by Zachary and Sherilyn Wilson

Printed and bound in China

For my dad, who taught me that
anything in life is possible.
You will be forever in my heart. xx

CONTENTS

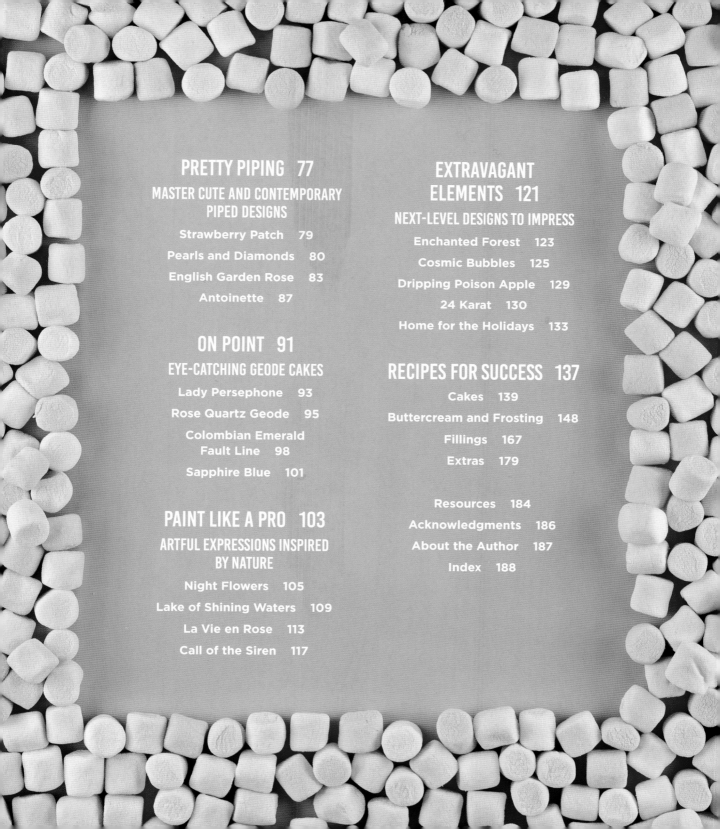

INTRODUCTION

Whether your goal is just to create a special cake for your little one's birthday party or you plan on becoming a full-fledged cake designer, my hope is that this book will not only become a source of inspiration for you, but also a comprehensive educational resource. There is so much to learn along the way, but I encourage you to take it one tutorial at a time. The chapters in this book are laid out in a progressive manner, so as you work your way through, you will quickly become better equipped to take on the next challenge.

The chapters are divided by techniques, with the simplest at the beginning and the more complex toward the end. Whether you want to learn the basics, practice your painting or master piping techniques, you'll find this book quick and easy to navigate. Throughout this book, you will use my tried-and-true base recipes—many of which have never been shared before now. Some of the simplest base recipes like the vanilla cake and buttercream frosting will also have instructions for making yummy flavor variations. This allows you to create custom flavor combinations for each cake tutorial. These recipes can be found in the Master the Basics (page 9) and Recipes for Success (page 137) chapters.

As you work through the book, I want you to have a "build your own" experience to help set you up to become a well-rounded baker while incorporating your own perspective and flair. You'll come to realize that most cake, buttercream and ganache recipes are built up from a base vanilla or chocolate recipe and are adjusted accordingly. You can mix and match flavors, colors and fillings to suit your taste. You will use almost all the techniques laid out in the Master the Basics chapter (page 9) as you work through the tutorials, so refer to it as much as you need to. The more you practice, the more confident you will become and the less time you'll spend getting the hang of the basics.

An amazing way to track your progress is with a photo journal. You can utilize such platforms as Facebook and Instagram to connect with other people who are just getting started as well! If you plan on using social media in any form to grow your business or even just to share your passion with family and friends, a backdrop or well-lit area for snapping photos and a pretty cake stand will be your best friends in achieving a gorgeous capture.

Above all else, I encourage you to bring your own creativity! After all, that is the main point of cake decorating. These tutorials were designed to guide you through the principles, but when it comes to personalization, let your imagination run wild! When learning anything new, you'll begin with imitation and slowly move into creating your own style later on. Trust the process and be kind to yourself—Rome wasn't built in a day!

Sheri Wilson

MASTER THE BASICS

This chapter goes over the fundamentals for best baking and decorating practices, as well as all the tricks I've learned throughout my own decorating journey. Practice as well as patience and lots of flexibility are key when it comes to cake decorating, or any form of artistic expression. Something important to learn early on is to embrace imperfections and find beauty in the process.

The techniques and recipes laid out in this chapter will assist you in learning the foundational principles needed to achieve the most successful (and tasty) results possible. You will find yourself referring to this chapter every step of the way as you hone those skills, so grab a bookmark and let's get started! I hope you are just as excited as I am!

TOOLS

Not a lot of tools are required for basic cake decorating, but the ones mentioned in this section will make your experience a lot more enjoyable and help you to achieve the best results. Besides the normal items in the kitchen, such as mixing bowls, measuring cups, pots and pans, knives and a good oven, here are the items used almost every time I decorate a cake.

Cake Pans

Most of the cakes in this book require four 6-inch (15-cm) or three 8-inch (20-cm) round layers per cake, which will obviously need to be baked in several batches if only two pans are available at a time. Four pans in each size are ideal, but work with what you have available and build from there. My favorite brands for cake pans are Wilton and Fat Daddio's. I'd recommend using the lighter-colored pans over the darker ones, as I've found they bake more evenly.

Cake Boards

A cake board larger than the cake itself is important for moving it around as well as for helping to secure it inside a cake box. Aim for a board 2 inches (5 cm) larger than the cake itself. My preference is acrylic boards, but they are available in cardboard as well. Find them at cake supply stores, Walmart and Amalfi Décor.

Offset Spatulas

An offset spatula is going to be one of your main tools, so you will want to purchase one that's decent quality. I love using Wilton's medium-sized offset spatula, as it has a firm handle, is very durable and can be washed in the dishwasher. Its small blade size is ideal for frosting small-to medium-sized cakes.

Tall Bench Scraper

Most bench scrapers are made of either acrylic or metal. I use both, but a metal scraper can be heated up before scraping, which makes it great for creating stripes. You can find metal combs and stripe combs online from Ester Cakes, and my brightly colored acrylic scrapers are from an Austria-based company called Zoi&Co. This is more about personal preference and neither one is necessarily better than the other.

Rubber Spatula

A stiff rubber spatula is essential in the kitchen for folding batter, mixing ingredients and scraping bowls. You can find these anywhere kitchen utensils are sold.

Turntable

A metal turntable is one of the basic tools you will need if you plan on decorating cakes beyond box mix in a sheet pan. They are easy to find on Amazon and are surprisingly affordable. A lazy Susan can also be used in a pinch.

Mixer

Most of the recipes in this book require the use of an electric mixer. If you do not have access to a stand mixer, an electric hand mixer will suffice; it may just take longer to prepare. If you are serious about baking and plan on turning it into a business or major hobby, a stand mixer is going to be the best thing you ever buy. I love the KitchenAid brand, as I'll mention more than once in this book, but many great mixers are available. Do your research and find out which suits your individual needs. Amazon is a great place to find most mixer models, but you can also find more specifics on the KitchenAid website.

Piping Tips and Bags

You don't need a lot of piping tips to get started, but I recommend a Wilton 2D, 1M, 1A and 6B for creating basic cake borders and executing the techniques used in this book. The nice thing is they can also be used for decorating cupcakes. Smaller, more intricate tips are so much fun to use and can be collected over time as you try out more techniques. Almost any piping bags will work, and depending on how thick they are, you may be able to wash and reuse them a few times.

Kitchen Scale

A kitchen scale is a vital tool when it comes to measuring and baking. Scales can be found at most stores that carry kitchen equipment.

Infrared Thermometer

A thermometer is an essential tool when making Italian meringue buttercream. I highly recommend an infrared thermometer over a clip-on thermometer, as it is so easy to use and is much more accurate, which is crucial for many recipes.

Oven Thermometer

An oven thermometer is key when it comes to baking. Many ovens bake at a different temperature than what they are set to, which is where a thermometer comes in handy to test accuracy. Every oven is different, so it is very helpful to be able to keep track of how long to bake something and at which temperature, according to your oven. Check your local grocery store to see whether it carries them.

Silicone Molds

You can sometimes purchase premade decorations, but most of the time it will be much more cost effective to make them yourself using molds. One I cannot recommend enough is a half-sphere mold, which you'll be able to find in several sizes. You can find a huge variety of molds at such places as Michaels, Jo-Ann, Walmart and Amazon.

Miscellaneous

A few other items that will make your life easier in the kitchen are cooling racks, a rolling pin, a hand whisk, cookie cutters, a fine-mesh sieve, parchment paper, dusting brushes and maybe a ruler.

CAKE BASICS
HOW TO MAKE A CAKE

Prepping Cake Pans

For most of the recipes in this book, you will need either 6-inch (15-cm) or 8-inch (20-cm) round cake pans. For the first couple of years of my baking journey, I had only one or two pans, and therefore had to bake the layers one at a time. This is doable if that is all you have available, but it can be very time consuming and a lot of effort. Especially if you plan on making a lot of cakes, having a set of four pans in each size is going to be a game changer!

1. To prepare each pan, begin by cutting out the parchment rounds to line the bottom. To cut out a parchment round, place your cake pan on a sheet of parchment paper and trace around it with a pen to mark out a circle. Cut it out and place in the bottom of the pan.

2. Generously spray the inside of each pan with vegetable oil spray. It doesn't need to be anything fancy—I've had the most success with the unflavored, boring, offbrand vegetable oil spray. Some varieties may cause extra browning on the crust, so experiment with different brands until you find one you like.

3. Next, place 1 to 2 tablespoons (8 to 16 g) of all-purpose flour (if preparing a vanilla-based cake) or unsweetened cocoa powder (if preparing a chocolate cake) into each cake pan and toss to coat. The flour or cocoa powder should completely coat the inside of the pan. Remove any excess flour or cocoa powder by lightly tapping the pans against a countertop. If using flour, pour the excess into a cup and reserve to use in a recipe later, if desired.

Preparing the Batter

My Classic Vanilla Cake recipe (page 15) is one you will see referenced a lot throughout this book, so you will become very familiar with it. Take your time and follow each instruction in this recipe for the best results. I use the reverse creaming method to prepare my vanilla cake, as I've found it to produce the fluffiest texture with a moist and tender crumb.

1A

1B

2

3

CLASSIC VANILLA CAKE

MAKES FOUR 6-INCH (15-CM) OR THREE 8-INCH (20-CM) ROUND CAKE LAYERS

The vanilla cake recipe of all cake recipes! Moist, fluffy and full of flavor—this cake is a staple for all bakers and pairs well with everything!

Vegetable oil spray, for pans

3 cups (375 g) all-purpose flour, plus more for dusting

3 cups (600 g) sugar

2 tsp (9 g) baking powder

3 tbsp (18 g) King Arthur cake enhancer (optional)

¾ tsp salt

1 cup (226 g) unsalted butter, at room temperature

3 large eggs, at room temperature

2 large egg whites, at room temperature

1½ cups (360 ml) buttermilk, at room temperature

2 tbsp (30 ml) sour cream, at room temperature

1 tbsp (15 ml) vanilla paste or pure vanilla extract

1. Preheat your oven to 350°F (176°C). Grease, dust with flour and line four 6-inch (15-cm) or three 8-inch (20-cm) round cake pans with parchment paper according to the directions on page 12.

2. Sift the flour, sugar, baking powder, cake enhancer (if using) and salt into the bowl of your stand mixer fitted with the paddle attachment. Set the mixer to the lowest speed and blend until well combined.

3. With the mixer still running on low speed, slowly add the butter to the bowl. Mix until fine crumbs have formed and no large clumps of butter remain.

4. In a medium-sized bowl, combine the eggs, egg whites, buttermilk, sour cream and vanilla paste and whisk to combine.

5. With the mixer on low, pour the wet ingredients into the bowl of your stand mixer in a slow and steady stream. Mix until just barely incorporated, scraping down the sides of the bowl when necessary. Increase the mixer speed to medium and beat until creamy—no longer than 1 to 2 minutes.

6. Divide the cake batter evenly among the prepared pans.

7. Bake for 30 to 35 minutes, or until a toothpick inserted into the center of a cake comes out clean and the cake has pulled away from the edges slightly. If the cakes are still raw on the inside, bake for an additional 3 to 5 minutes while keeping a close eye on them to avoid overbaking. Remove the pans from the oven and allow the cakes to cool in their pans for approximately 15 minutes before inverting them onto wire racks or a clean countertop. Allow the layers to cool completely.

8. Using a large, serrated knife, level the top and trim the caramelization (the golden brown outer crust) from each layer. Wrap the cake layers in plastic wrap and chill for a minimum of 3 to 4 hours in the fridge or 30 minutes in the freezer before stacking and decorating.

TIP

- This recipe can easily be used for baking cupcakes. Pour the prepared batter into a cupcake tray (or trays) and bake for 18 to 21 minutes, or until a toothpick inserted in the center of one comes out clean. Makes about 48 cupcakes.

FLAVOR VARIATIONS

Chocolate Chip Cake

Prepare the Classic Vanilla Cake batter. Fold 1 cup (170 g) of semisweet chocolate chips into the batter, and bake as directed.

Funfetti Cake

Prepare the Classic Vanilla Cake batter. Fold 1 cup (200 g) of rainbow sprinkles into the batter, and bake as directed.

Cookies & Cream Cake

Prepare the Classic Vanilla Cake batter, and fold 20 crushed chocolate sandwich cookies into the batter. Bake as directed.

Cherry Swirl Cake

Prepare the Classic Vanilla Cake batter and divide equally among the pans. Scoop ½ cup (133 g) of Cherry Filling (page 168) into each pan and swirl through the batter using a toothpick. Bake as directed.

Toasted Coconut Cake

Prepare the Classic Vanilla Cake batter and add 1 to 2 teaspoons (5 to 10 ml) of Get Suckered Toasted Coconut flavoring or coconut extract in addition to the vanilla paste when preparing. Fold in 1 cup (85 g) of unsweetened shredded coconut. Bake as directed.

Bubblegum Cake

Prepare the Classic Vanilla Cake batter and add 10 drops of Chefmaster pink gel coloring. Add 1 to 2 teaspoons (5 to 10 ml) of Get Suckered Bubblegum flavoring in addition to the vanilla paste when preparing. Bake as directed.

Peppermint Cake

Prepare the Classic Vanilla Cake batter and fold in 1 cup (240 g) of crushed candy canes. Add 1 teaspoon of peppermint extract in addition to the vanilla paste when preparing. Bake as directed.

Pink Strawberry Cake

Prepare the Classic Vanilla Cake batter, adding 4 drops of Chefmaster pink gel coloring and 1 to 2 teaspoons (5 to 10 ml) of Get Suckered strawberry flavoring or strawberry extract in addition to the vanilla paste when preparing. Fold in 1 cup (20 g) of powdered freeze-dried strawberries. Bake as directed.

Cherry Chip Cake

Prepare the Classic Vanilla Cake batter, adding 4 drops of Chefmaster pink gel coloring and 1 to 2 teaspoons (5 to 10 ml) of almond extract in addition to the vanilla paste when preparing. Fold in 1 cup (161 g) of chopped and drained maraschino cherries and 1 cup (170 g) of mini chocolate chips. Bake as directed.

Raspberry Cake

Prepare the Classic Vanilla Cake batter, adding 5 drops of Chefmaster pink gel coloring and 1 to 2 teaspoons (5 to 10 ml) of Get Suckered raspberry flavoring or raspberry extract in addition to the vanilla paste when preparing. Fold in 1 cup (20 g) of powdered freeze-dried raspberries. Bake as directed.

Cranberry Orange Cake

Toss 2 cups (220 g) of fresh cranberries in powdered sugar to coat, shaking off any excess. Prepare the Classic Vanilla Cake batter and fold in the coated cranberries and the zest of 2 large oranges. Bake as directed.

CAKE STORAGE

Decorating a cake will always be a lot less daunting if all the components have already been prepared ahead of time. This is why freezing cake layers for later use is extremely helpful, especially if you have a lot of cake orders to fit into a short amount of time. Wrapped cake layers will keep in the refrigerator for up to 3 days, or in the freezer for 1 to 2 months. When ready to use, remove from the freezer, allow the layers to thaw slightly in the refrigerator and decorate while still cold.

TIPS FOR BAKING SUCCESS

- Consider the baking temperatures and times mentioned in this book as a starting point. Every oven is different, and their heating abilities vary greatly. Therefore, it's important to get to know your own oven. Use a thermometer to gauge the temperature during bake time and adjust accordingly.

- Add King Arthur cake enhancer to your batter for a super-fluffy cake texture.

- Carefully measure (or better yet, weigh) your ingredients and follow the recipe instructions! This seems like a no-brainer, but it can be easy to try to take shortcuts in the kitchen, especially when you're short on time. This is not one that should be taken. Each recipe is specifically formulated to work based on the instructions and measurements provided. Once you become more confident in the kitchen and understand the science behind how recipes work, have fun experimenting with switching up flavors, but it will always remain important to follow the recipe instructions and use the correct measurements. This will also help you achieve consistently successful results.

- Sift your dry ingredients. This not only eliminates lumps, but also helps aerate dry ingredients.

- Always start with room-temperature ingredients. This will help the batter blend together correctly and prevent dense spots in your cake. You can easily bring butter and milk to room temperature by microwaving them in a microwave-safe bowl for 15 to 20 seconds. Eggs can be placed into a bowl of warm water until they have reached room temperature. If your batter appears curdled and separated, it is most likely because your ingredients were too cold when you started.

- Be sure to check your cake for doneness before removing it from the oven to prevent it from sinking in the middle. Sinking may also happen if the oven door was opened too often during baking (guilty here). Try your best to resist the urge to constantly open the door and instead use the light in your oven to check.

Wrapped cake layers

- Always make sure your leavening agents (such as baking powder and baking soda) are fresh and well sealed. You would be surprised how common it is to accidentally use expired leavening!

- If your cake layers are coming out browned and crispy on top, try lowering the temperature of your oven. They are either baking for too long or the temperature is too high.

BUTTERCREAM BASICS

This is the simplest and most often used buttercream in this book and is the perfect place to start when first learning how to decorate cakes. My Simple Vanilla Buttercream recipe on the next page creates an American-style buttercream, which only uses a few ingredients and doesn't require any cooking or special equipment. Naturally, it is a very sweet buttercream, but by adding a touch of lemon juice, the sweetness becomes a lot more balanced. American buttercream is a crusting buttercream, which means it will form a dry outer layer after sitting for a time. Other types of buttercream, such as Swiss or Italian meringue, do not crust; rather, they stay wet and tacky to the touch. This crusting buttercream is amazing to paint onto or pipe with and holds its shape well.

SIMPLE VANILLA BUTTER-CREAM

MAKES APPROXIMATELY 6 CUPS (1.8 KG)

American buttercream is the simplest buttercream to make out of all of them! I use this recipe on a daily basis and love how versatile it is for decorating!

---

1 cup (226 g) unsalted butter, at room temperature

1 cup (205 g) vegetable shortening, at room temperature

½ cup (120 ml) heavy cream

1 tbsp (15 ml) pure vanilla extract (or clear vanilla extract if white buttercream is desired)

Pinch of salt

2 tbsp (30 ml) fresh lemon juice (optional)

2 lb (907 g) powdered sugar, sifted

1. In the bowl of your stand mixer fitted with the paddle attachment, combine the butter and shortening and beat on high speed for 5 minutes, or until very pale and the mixture has increased in volume.

2. Set your mixer to its lowest speed and add the heavy cream, vanilla and salt. Add the lemon juice to reduce the sweetness, if desired.

3. Begin adding the powdered sugar, 1 cup (120 g) at a time, until all has been added. Beat at medium speed until the buttercream is smooth and creamy—no longer than 1 to 2 minutes, or else excess air bubbles will form.

4. Allow your mixer to run at the lowest setting for about 5 minutes. Remove any remaining bubbles by pressing the buttercream against the side of the bowl. You should hear a popping sound as the bubbles come to the surface and burst. Continue scraping and folding by hand until the buttercream is very smooth and no visible bubbles remain. This can take quite a while sometimes, depending on how much air was incorporated into the buttercream when whipping. Take your time, and don't be afraid to take a breather if your arm is falling off from beating!

This buttercream can be stored for up to 2 weeks in the refrigerator or 1 month in the freezer. Allow the buttercream to come to room temperature and rewhip on medium speed before using.

SUBSTITUTIONS

Vegetable shortening helps balance out the flavor of the butter and will produce a much whiter buttercream, and it's also more stable in warmer climates. Feel free to omit the shortening and use all butter, if preferred. If using all butter, reduce the amount of heavy cream to ⅓ cup (80 ml), as butter contains a lot more moisture than shortening.

TIPS

- Try some of the flavor variations with the Italian Meringue Buttercream recipe on page 152 if you prefer a less sweet buttercream than used here. Use the same measurements as listed here when preparing a flavor variation.

- If a tutorial calls for ½ batch of buttercream, simply halve all the ingredients and prepare as directed.

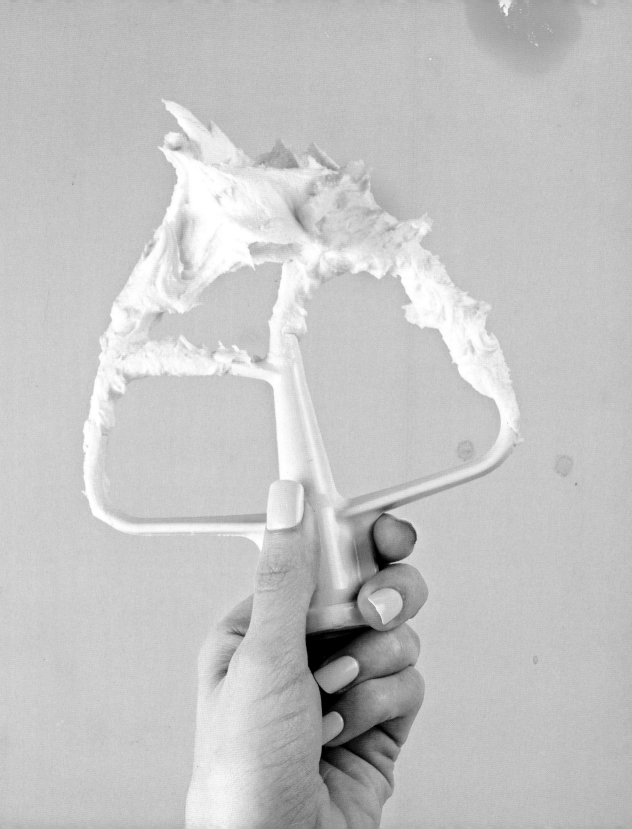

FLAVOR VARIATIONS

Anise Buttercream

Prepare the Simple Vanilla Buttercream, replacing ½ teaspoon of the vanilla with ½ teaspoon of anise extract.

Orange Sherbet Buttercream

Prepare the Simple Vanilla Buttercream, replacing 1 teaspoon of the vanilla with 1 teaspoon of Get Suckered Orange Creamsicle flavoring.

Bubblegum Buttercream

Prepare the Simple Vanilla Buttercream, replacing 1 teaspoon of the vanilla with 1 teaspoon of Get Suckered Bubblegum flavoring.

Baileys Buttercream

Prepare the Simple Vanilla Buttercream, replacing the heavy cream with Baileys Irish Cream.

Peppermint Buttercream

Prepare the Simple Vanilla Buttercream, adding 1 teaspoon of peppermint extract in addition to the vanilla extract.

Cookies & Cream Buttercream

Prepare the Simple Vanilla Buttercream and fold in 20 crushed chocolate sandwich cookies.

BUTTERCREAM STORAGE

Make your buttercream ahead of time to streamline your decorating process and store it in the fridge or freezer until ready to use. American buttercream is shelf stable for up to 3 days, but should be refrigerated beyond that to ensure freshness. Transfer to large ziplock bags and store in the fridge for up to 1 week, or in the freezer for up to 1 month. When ready to use, bring it to room temperature, rewhip on medium-low speed for a few minutes and it is all set!

TIPS FOR BUTTERCREAM SUCCESS

Learning how to master buttercream is the key to having success when decorating a cake. The most important things to keep in mind regarding buttercream are consistency, temperature and aeration. If you are just starting out, I highly recommend learning to decorate using my Simple Vanilla Buttercream (page 18) before trying my Italian Meringue Buttercream (page 152). It is much more forgiving and easier to work with at first. Meringue-based buttercreams taste amazing, but do require extra equipment and practice to perfect. The following tips, tricks and techniques mostly refer to American buttercream, but the basic principles remain the same for any variety. Refer to page 156 for tips specifically tailored to perfecting Italian meringue.

Medium-firm consistency buttercream

Soft-medium consistency buttercream

CONSISTENCY

Buttercream should have a consistency similar to that of toothpaste, but the overall consistency can be very easily adjusted to suit your needs. Depending on the project, you will use different consistencies of buttercream to achieve different designs. To adjust your buttercream to be thinner, add 1 to 2 tablespoons (15 to 30 ml) of heavy cream at a time until the desired consistency is reached. To thicken it up, add approximately ¼ cup (25 g) of sifted powdered sugar at a time until the desired consistency is reached.

Piping Consistency

To pipe dimensional designs, such as flowers, cacti or fine details, you will use a medium- to firm-consistency buttercream. These types of designs need to hold their shape when piped, as well as crust when placed at room temperature. Using less heavy cream when making your buttercream will cause it to crust more quickly, whereas

using more heavy cream results in a very soft crust or no crust at all. This has to do with how much moisture is in the buttercream. Less moisture equals faster drying time; more moisture equals longer drying time. If you have piped a flower or a swirl and the buttercream has drooped down, that is a clear indication that it is not thick enough. If the buttercream refuses to come out of the piping tip and it is difficult to squeeze, it is most likely too thick. Be sure to also take the temperature of the buttercream into consideration, as this makes a huge difference—more about that follows.

Cake Icing Consistency

To frost the surface of a cake, you will use a soft- to medium-consistency buttercream. It needs to be firm enough to stay in place while spreading onto the cake, but not so soft that it runs or melts down while smoothing. This is also the ideal consistency for basic piping for line work, dots, rosettes, borders and edging.

TEMPERATURE

Temperature plays a huge role in buttercream and is something you will have to keep in mind during the decorating, storing and serving stages. Think about buttercream the way you would think about a stick of butter; after all, butter is one of its main ingredients. The warmer it gets, the runnier it becomes and it can even completely liquefy if warm enough. As soon as it heats up, the texture thins out and it separates. If butter is taken directly out of the fridge or has been in a cold room, it will be firm and difficult to spread. We are aiming for a perfect medium: cool enough that it would glide across a piece of toast without breaking the bread, but not melting off the knife and getting your hands greasy. You can easily change the temperature of the buttercream by placing your bowl or piping bag in the refrigerator or freezer until it has firmed up or by placing it in a warm area (maybe near the stove) until it is malleable.

AERATION

You will notice that if you whip buttercream for an extended period of time, it will have a lot more bubbles in it and will not appear very smooth and pasty. You do beat the butter and shortening together until increased in volume and very fluffy, but avoid incorporating air into the buttercream after this point, as the texture will be very difficult to smooth.

Mix your buttercream on low speed while making it, not only to prevent a powdered sugar dust storm from your mixer, but also to prevent extra air bubbles from forming. You can leave your mixer running on low speed for 5 to 10 minutes to help work out any air bubbles as well. I ultimately prefer doing this by hand as you have a little more control of the overall consistency and texture. I'm also impatient and normally want to use the buttercream ASAP! To eliminate air bubbles by hand, simply press the buttercream against the sides of the bowl using a rubber spatula. You should hear some popping sounds as the air bubbles come to the surface. If you are having a very difficult time achieving smooth buttercream, place the bowl in the freezer for 10 to 15 minutes and mix again. Sometimes changing the temperature is all that is needed to make it smooth and creamy.

GANACHE DRIP BASICS

Ganache drips are a very popular decoration on buttercream cakes and are simple to achieve, given a little bit of practice. These drips are created using a thinned ganache of either white or dark chocolate, sometimes with added gel coloring to create a brightly colored drip. It may take a little bit of practice to perfect, but with the right recipe, you will be well on your way to success! Something I cannot stress enough is to use high-quality chocolate. The higher the quality, the more consistent results you will have. I love using Ghirardelli chocolate chips to create ganache drips.

MILK OR DARK CHOCOLATE GANACHE DRIP

MAKES APPROXIMATELY 1 CUP (240 ML) GANACHE

Chocolate ganache drips are a delicious and simple way to dress up any cake. Use milk chocolate for a balanced flavor or dark chocolate for something more robust. Ganache drips only require two ingredients, so there's no need to feel intimidated when using this simple microwave method.

1 cup (170 g) milk or dark chocolate chips (I prefer Ghirardelli)

¾ cup (180 ml) heavy cream

1. In a microwave-safe container, combine the milk or dark chocolate and heavy cream. Microwave for 30-second intervals, gently stirring in between, until completely melted.

2. Once completely melted, stir gently until the ganache is smooth.

3. Cover and allow the ganache to reach room temperature before using it on a cake.

Store unused ganache in an airtight container in the refrigerator for up to 1 week. Allow it to return to room temperature or reheat in the microwave to return it to a more fluid consistency.

COLOR VARIATION

Midnight Black Drip

Prepare the Dark Chocolate Ganache Drip recipe, adding 4 to 6 drops of black gel coloring after it is completely melted. Stir until the color is well incorporated.

WHITE CHOCOLATE GANACHE DRIP

MAKES APPROXIMATELY ¾ CUP (180 ML) GANACHE

My go-to white chocolate ganache recipe—this is perfect for creating a white or colored drip, and works every time!

1 cup (170 g) white chocolate chips (I prefer Ghirardelli)

¼ cup (60 ml) heavy cream

Wilton whitener gel

GANACHE DRIP TIPS

- Be sure not to incorporate a lot of air into the ganache when stirring; these bubbles will be visible in the final product.

- Feel free to leave out the whitener gel if a bright white color is not required.

- Avoid using such products as candy melts to ensure a great flavor and consistency.

1. In a microwave-safe container, combine the white chocolate and heavy cream, and microwave in 30-second intervals, gently stirring in between, until completely melted.

2. Once completely melted, add the whitener gel and gently stir until the gel has been well incorporated.

3. Cover loosely with plastic wrap and allow the ganache to cool to room temperature before using it on a cake.

Store unused ganache in an airtight container in the refrigerator for up to 1 week. Allow it to return to room temperature or reheat in the microwave to return it to a more fluid consistency.

COLOR VARIATION

Brightly Colored Drip

Prepare the White Chocolate Ganache Drip recipe, adding 2 to 5 drops of your desired gel coloring after the chocolate and cream are completely melted. Stir until the color is well incorporated.

Runny

Thick

Just right

TIPS FOR GANACHE DRIP SUCCESS

To test whether your ganache has reached the correct consistency, drip it onto a glass first and watch how far it reaches. It really depends on the aesthetic you are shooting for, but I like the drips to reach about halfway down my cake. If the drip runs off the glass, it is still too warm, or you might have added too much heavy cream.

If it barely forms a drip and just pools around the edge, it doesn't have enough heavy cream or has set for too long.

It is ideal for the drip to reach about halfway to three-quarters of the way down the glass.

To Thicken Ganache

Either let it sit for a longer period of time to firm up or add extra melted chocolate, ¼ cup (60 ml) at a time.

To Thin Ganache

Simply add extra heavy cream, a teaspoon at a time, and place back in the microwave for 15 to 20 seconds to reheat.

Piping bag/bottle method

Spoon method

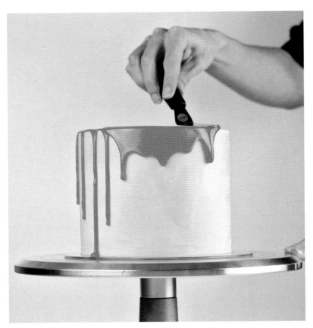

Curtain method

DRIPPING TECHNIQUES

There are lots of different methods to add drips to a cake and you will soon adopt your favorite, but here are some you can start with. With any method, you can control the length of the drips by applying more or less ganache to certain areas. Feel free to cover the entire top of the cake in ganache, or simply apply it to the very edge of the cake. A lot of the time, the center will be covered with other decorations, such as sprinkles or frosting, so it is not always necessary to cover completely.

Piping Bag/Bottle Method

Transfer the prepared ganache to a piping bag or drip bottle and apply drips along the top edge of the cake.

Spoon Method

Using a teaspoon, drizzle ganache onto the top edge of the cake.

Curtain Method

Pour the ganache onto the top of the cake, and with an offset spatula, push the ganache toward the edge, allowing the ganache to flow over it (my personal favorite).

Adding buttercream to the piping bag

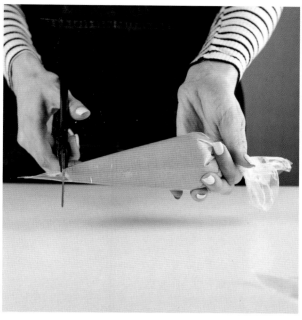

Tipless method

Tip method

TECHNIQUE BASICS
HOW TO FILL A PIPING BAG

Tipless Method

1. Place a piping bag into a tall glass, folding the excess plastic over the edges of the glass.

2. Transfer the buttercream or filling into the bag using a rubber spatula, pressing down to avoid trapping air pockets inside the bag. Leave 4 to 5 inches (10 to 13 cm) of free space at the open end after adding the filling, so you have ample room to hold and maneuver the piping bag.

3. Unfold the end and lift the filled bag out of the glass. Twist the end twice to prevent the filling from spilling out of the bag and snip 1 inch (2.5 cm) from the end using sharp scissors.

Tip Method

1. Line up the piping tip with the end of the bag and mark a line where the base is. Snip off the end along the line you marked and insert the tip, then follow steps 1 to 3 of the Tipless Method.

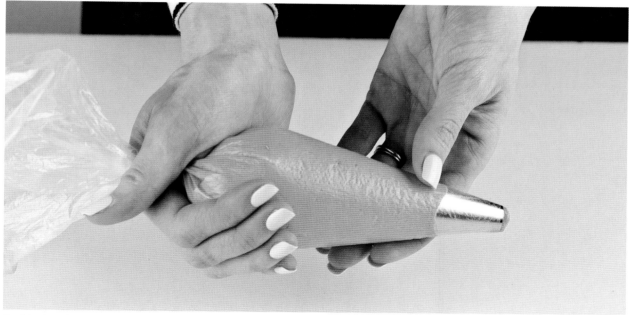

Positioning the piping bag

Tip

Be sure the grooves of the tip are not covered by the bag at all. If there is any overhang, simply remove the tip and cut a little more from the end of the piping bag. You can always take more off, but once you've cut too much, there isn't a lot you can do but use a new bag.

HOW TO HOLD A PIPING BAG

Position the end of the piping bag in the palm of your hand, pinching the tail firmly between your thumb and pointer finger. Squeeze from the top of the bag down, keeping the opening closed using your thumb and pointer finger. Using a piping bag takes a lot of practice, so don't worry if it takes a few tries to get the hang of how to hold it comfortably. It also takes some hand and wrist muscle, which is developed over time.

Piping Bag Tips

- If the buttercream inside your piping bag seems runny or separated, it may be too warm from being handled. Place the entire bag in the refrigerator for 10 to 15 minutes to solidify. Knead after chilling and reuse.

- If your buttercream seems stuck in the bag, there may be a clump jammed inside the piping tip. Most of the time, you will be able to fish it out using a toothpick or cookie scribe.

- Avoid overfilling the piping bag, or else you are likely to get buttercream all over your hands. It's better to add extra buttercream in stages if more is needed.

- If you are only using a piping bag to fill or frost a cake in a tutorial, I do not list the amount of piping bags needed in the tools list. If you use multiple piping bags to create the design, then I note the amount needed in the tools list.

HOW TO BUILD A CAKE

The following techniques will work when building a cake with any type of buttercream, but are best suited for American buttercream. If you're using a meringue-based buttercream to decorate with, I suggest using the fridge instead of the freezer to chill your cake, as extreme temperature changes can cause the buttercream to separate. For meringue-based buttercream, use a cool but not completely cold cake during the decorating process.

Filling and Stacking—Classic Method

1. Prepare your buttercream and transfer about 2 cups (600 g) to a piping bag with the end snipped off. Have your cake layers prepped and chilled.

2. If using a nonstick mat, place it onto your turntable. This is recommended, as it will prevent the cake from moving around while frosting. In a pinch, you could stick the cake board to the turntable using a piece of tape.

3. Place the cake board on top of the nonstick mat on the turntable. Your cake board should be a little bit larger than the cake itself.

4. With your piping bag, squeeze a small amount (1 to 2 tablespoons [20 to 40 g]) of buttercream onto the center of the cake board. This will help the layers stick to the board while frosting.

5. Place the first layer on the board, leveled side up, and press on the cake to secure it.

6. Holding your piping bag at a 45-degree angle in the center of the cake layer, pipe a spiral, moving outward. The goal is to create a thin, even layer of buttercream on the cake.

7. Hold an offset spatula stationary while rotating the turntable counterclockwise to smooth out the buttercream. (If right-handed; if left-handed, rotate clockwise.)

8. Place a second layer of cake, leveled side up, on top of the frosted layer and press down to secure.

9. Add a layer of buttercream to the second cake layer, the same way you applied it the first time, smoothing with your offset spatula.

10. Repeat this a third time, placing the third layer of cake, leveled side up, on top of the second and adding a third layer of buttercream.

11. Place the fourth and final layer of cake on top of the third frosted layer, this time flipping it so the leveled side is facedown. This will help to trap in crumbs while frosting. Check that each layer is completely lined up and is sitting level. You can test whether they are lined up by placing the tall bench scraper against the cake as a guide. Adjust any layers, if necessary.

8A

8B

9

10

Filling and Stacking—Dam Method

1. Prepare your buttercream and transfer to a piping bag with the end snipped off, about 2 cups (600 g) total.

2. Prepare your filling and transfer it to a piping bag with the end snipped off, about 1 cup (300 g) total.

3. Place the cake board on top of the nonstick mat on the turntable. Your board should be a little bit larger than the cake itself. With your piping bag, squeeze a small amount (1 to 2 tablespoons [20 to 40 g]) of buttercream onto the center of the cake board; this will help the layers stick to the board while frosting.

4. Place the first layer of cake, leveled side up, onto the board and press on the top to secure it.

5. Holding your piping bag at a 45-degree angle to the cake layer, pipe a thick "dam" or "wall" of buttercream around the outer edge. This dam will prevent the filling from oozing out of the cake.

6. Fill the center of the layer (inside the dam) with filling. Be sure the height of the filling does not exceed that of the buttercream. It is important not to overfill the layers during this process, as it could cause your cake to shift or even collapse. About ¼ cup (75 g) or less is the ideal amount of filling between each layer.

7. Place a layer of cake, leveled side up, on top of the frosted layer and gently press on the top to secure.

8. Pipe a dam of buttercream along the edge of the second layer, the same way you applied it the first time, adding the filling in the center.

9. Repeat this a third time, placing a third layer of cake, leveled side up, on top of the second layer, adding a dam of buttercream along the edge as well as the filling in the center.

10. Place the fourth and final layer of cake on top of the third frosted layer, this time flipping it so the leveled side is facedown. This will help to trap in crumbs while frosting. Check that each layer is completely lined up and is sitting level. You can test whether they are lined up by placing the tall bench scraper against the cake as a guide. Adjust any layers, if necessary.

Cake Building Tips

- Depending on how stable your cake is after filling, you may want to transfer it to the fridge or freezer until well chilled and stable enough to frost. Sometimes I let a cake settle in the refrigerator for 3 to 4 hours after filling using the dam method to ensure it is firm and stable. This is not always necessary, but can be very helpful depending on how runny your fillings are, as well as the temperature of your kitchen.

- It is important to gently but firmly press down on the top of the cake while stacking to make sure no air is trapped in between the layers. As the cake warms up to room temperature before serving, the air inside will expand and may cause unsightly pockets or bubbles under the surface of the buttercream or frosting.

Crumb Coat Step 1 *Crumb Coat Step 2* *Final Coat Step 1* *Final Coat Step 5*

CRUMB COAT

1. After you finish stacking and filling your cake, apply the crumb coat using the remaining buttercream in your piping bag. Evenly apply it all over the cake. If you do not have enough buttercream left in the piping bag to completely cover it, add more with the offset spatula.

2. Smooth out the buttercream using a tall bench scraper, taking care to cover the entire surface of the cake in a thin layer. The smoother you can make it, the better, but this is just an undercoat and it does not have to look pretty. The main goal is to trap in all the crumbs and prevent their getting into the final coat.

3. Once the cake is completely covered, transfer to the freezer to chill for approximately 20 minutes, or in the refrigerator for 3 to 4 hours. This layer of buttercream needs to be cold before adding the next layer or you will not have a firm surface to work upon.

FINAL COAT

1. Once well chilled, return the crumb-coated cake to the turntable. Dollop 1 to 2 cups (300 to 600 g) of the remaining buttercream onto the very top. With your spatula, spread the buttercream all over the cake, creating a thick and even coat. It is very important to make sure the coating is applied evenly over the entire surface, or the cake may begin to look small at the bottom and wider at the top, or vice versa.

2. Hold the bench scraper vertically against the cake at a 45-degree angle and begin to scrape. Clean off the scraper after each full rotation.

3. Reapply extra buttercream to any areas lacking coverage, continuing to keep the buttercream even and lined up from the top to the bottom. Allow the buttercream to build up along the top edge as you scrape, making it level with the sides of the cake. We will cut this edge off with a knife at the end. Continue to scrape until the surface is as smooth as you can manage.

4. Place your cake back in the freezer to chill for an additional 20 minutes.

5. Once chilled, take a sharp knife and run it along the top edge of the cake, cutting off the lip of excess buttercream. This will form a sharp top edge. Place the cake back in the refrigerator to stay cool while you prepare your decorations.

BEAUTY COAT

This step is optional, but I've found it to make such a difference in the end result and would suggest trying it if you struggled to achieve a smooth final coat. Skip straight to decorating if you aren't applying the beauty coat.

1. Return the cake to the turntable and apply a third and final "beauty coat." This is a very thin coat applied to the cold and firm frosted cake to help get rid of any remaining imperfections and cover any blemishes. Apply the buttercream to the cake with either the offset spatula or a piping bag.

2. Scrape smooth using the tall bench scraper. Because the cake is completely cold and firm, the buttercream applied to the surface will change slightly and become more pastelike in consistency. This is an ideal consistency to achieve a clean and smooth finish.

Cake Frosting Tips

*   If you are seeing lots of little air bubbles while scraping, be sure to fold the air out of your buttercream with a rubber spatula before using; this will cause the buttercream to become smooth and silky, and it will be much easier to work with.

*   If the layer of buttercream you are working on is pulling away the layer beneath, it is probably time to rechill the cake.

*   If your cake forms small droplets of water or condensation on the surface, it is most likely due to drastic temperature changes. Always aim to work in a cool environment when using buttercream or crank up your air-conditioning as much as possible, if available. Heat is buttercream's worst enemy. In the summertime, or if you live in a very warm or humid climate, it may be better to only use the refrigerator, as the freezer may cause too drastic a temperature change. The weather is something that needs to be factored in if it is an issue, and perhaps plan your decorating schedule around the coolest parts of the day. If using the freezer, be careful not to leave the cake in for longer than 20 minutes, or it could become completely frozen. Chilling in the freezer is only intended to chill the outer layer until firm; any longer is likely to cause the cake to "sweat," or form condensation, as soon as it hits room temperature. To eliminate excess moisture, gently dab with a paper towel and place in the refrigerator overnight. Most of the condensation will be gone by morning.

*   You may need to apply extra buttercream around the top edge and base after scraping. These areas are more structurally compromised than the middle and will take extra effort to level.

HOW TO STACK TIERED CAKES

Stacking cakes may seem scary, but I'm here to help simplify the process and you'll find it is probably much easier than you imagined. I'm all for expanding your boundaries and trying something new, but I would suggest perfecting single-tier cake-building before attempting to stack tiers. The most important thing to keep in mind when creating multitiered cakes is stability and structure. That means your cakes need to be completely level and well chilled for you to be able to move them around with ease. The general rule of thumb for picking the sizes is to use a cake 2 inches (5 cm) smaller in diameter than the one beneath it; for instance, a base cake of 8 inches (20 cm) with a top cake of 6 inches (15 cm), and so on. The size is completely up to you, but this is my personal preference. You can also experiment with how tall each tier is for a completely different look. I've found taller or thinner tiers have more of a modern look, whereas shorter or wider tiers are preferable for a more traditional-style cake.

1. Start with very cold, buttercream-frosted cakes. You should be able to handle them without damaging the buttercream at all. Place a bubble tea straw against the side of a cake and mark the height onto it.

2. Cut four straws to the same length. The straws will create the structural support for the cake above it, so be sure they are all cut straight.

3. Press the straws in a square formation into the largest (base) cake. If needed, you can mark the center of the cake with a ruler to use as a guide when inserting the straws. Be sure they go in straight and sit completely level with the top of the cake as well as reach all the way down to the bottom. To make them easier to insert, you can press them down the last little bit by using your offset spatula.

4. The top cake layer will need to have a cardboard disk under it, the same size as the cake itself, so it will not be seen when stacked. Place a cake lifter or spatula under the smaller cake and using your other hand to balance, place it on top of the larger cake, centered on top of the straws.

5. Apply extra buttercream to any blemishes or holes and smooth with your offset spatula. Place the cake into the fridge, allowing it to chill and settle.

Tip

- If desired, a long wooden dowel can be inserted into the top of the cake and pushed all the way down until it reaches the base cake board. This is not always necessary but will provide an extra level of stability. Be sure to measure the dowel and cut it to the proper length before inserting.

HOW TO CUT A CAKE

1. Cutting a tall cake can be a little tricky sometimes! Always start with a cold cake, if possible. Have a cutting board ready to hold up to the side of the cake, and with a sharp knife, cut a 1-inch (2.5-cm) slice from the side.

2. Allow the slice to lean against the cutting board, lay it down and cut the slice in half or into thirds directly on the board.

3. Transfer to individual plates for serving. This method will create the perfect party-sized slice and will also produce a lot more servings than the regular method of slicing a cake.

4. These slices can easily be transferred to a large container and refrigerated. It is best if eaten within 3 days, or frozen for up to 2 months. Remove from the refrigerator or freezer and bring to room temperature before serving.

Tip

*   It is always best to keep cakes chilled until about 1 hour before serving, and when possible, to cut while cold to create clean and easy slices.

TRAVELING WITH CAKES

It is never a good idea to leave a cake in a warm area or you may just end up with a melted puddle instead of a beautifully decorated masterpiece. I didn't know this when I first started out decorating and would take cakes on long trips without any air-conditioning in the car. The results were very disappointing and I learned quickly that buttercream cakes require refrigeration. Traveling with prechilled cakes in an air-conditioned vehicle is a lot safer, as they will be more stable. Be sure to bring a kit of extra buttercream, decorations, a scraper, piping tips and an offset spatula in case you run into an emergency. It's always better to be prepared than to arrive at a venue with a damaged cake. Always place cakes on top of a flat surface in a box the same size as the board to prevent them from sliding around while transporting.

Keeping taller cakes chilled is even more important because their structure is not as solid as a short cake. A tall cake can shift, which may result in air pockets and leaning. It is best to keep cakes cold for as long as possible; cut while cold and serve after 30 minutes to an hour. I'd suggest using ganache to cover a cake if it needs to sit out for a long period of time for something like a wedding or a party. Ganache does not melt the same way buttercream does and has a much firmer consistency once set.

If traveling for long distances with multitiered cakes, you may want to invest in a cake-safe box. These boxes come in many sizes and have a supporting rod through the middle, which prevents the cake from moving around. Most small single-tier cakes will be just fine in a snugly fit cake box in the backseat or trunk of the vehicle.

SPRINKLE CLUB

EASY-PEASY SPRINKLE ART

Sprinkles have come a long way since the days of ice cream toppings and cheap grocery store confetti cakes! You can now find deluxe sprinkles in every color and theme imaginable. Sprinkles have made a huge debut in the cake world in recent years and are now a staple of most buttercream cake artists. Using sprinkles is a great place to begin, as they do most of the decorating work for you. If you're stuck on the design or which colors to use, simply apply the same color palette and theme of the sprinkle blend to the cake you're making. They can add a huge amount of pizzazz as well as a tasty crunch to any dessert. There are so many creative ways to use a good old bottle of sprinkles, which you'll witness firsthand throughout this chapter!

READY TO PARTY

MAKES ONE 6-INCH (15-CM), 4-LAYER ROUND CAKE

SERVES 10 TO 12

I think we can all agree that the cake is a central part of every birthday party! This happy cake has fluffy Chocolate Chip Cake layers, is filled with Edible Cookie Dough and frosted in Simple Vanilla Buttercream. Because this is the very first cake of the book, we will begin with a simple design. It may not use any elaborate techniques, but a classic buttercream drip cake will always hold a special place in my heart. Disclaimer: This cake has been known to have everyone coming back for seconds, so don't forget to save yourself a slice!

1 batch Chocolate Chip Cake (page 16)

1 batch Edible Cookie Dough (page 179)

1 batch Simple Vanilla Buttercream (page 18)

Chefmaster sky blue, lemon yellow and pink gel coloring

1 batch White Chocolate Ganache Drip (page 24)

¼ cup (40 g) Sprinkle Pop "Rainbow Beam" sprinkles

2 tbsp (26 g) rainbow nonpareil sprinkles

8 stemmed maraschino cherries, drained

Candles (optional)

TOOLS

Parchment paper

Rolling pin

Wilton 1M piping tip

Large baking sheet

PREP

1. Prepare the Chocolate Chip Cake, making four 6-inch (15-cm) cake layers, and Edible Cookie Dough.

2. Place a sheet of parchment paper on a flat surface. Use a 6-inch (15-cm) pan to trace two circles onto the parchment.

3. Divide the cookie dough in half and roll each half into a ball using your hands. Place each dough ball on a traced circle and, using the rolling pin, roll until the dough has formed a disk as large as the circle you traced, approximately ¼ inch (6 mm) in thickness. Cut off any excess with a knife. With the cookie dough still on the parchment paper, slide onto a cookie sheet and place in the fridge to chill until firm.

4. Prepare the Simple Vanilla Buttercream. Place 1 cup (300 g) of the buttercream in a small bowl and add 3 to 4 drops of sky blue gel coloring. Transfer the blue buttercream to a piping bag fitted with a 1M tip. This will be used to pipe the swirls on top of the cake.

5. Color the remaining buttercream in your stand mixer bowl with 5 drops of lemon yellow gel coloring. Cover and set aside—this will be used to final coat the cake.

6. Prepare the White Chocolate Ganache Drip. While the ganache is still warm, add 3 to 5 drops of pink gel coloring. Stir gently until the color is well incorporated. Cover and set aside until ready to use.

ASSEMBLY

7. Prepare to fill and stack your cake using the classic method detailed on page 30. After placing the first cake layer onto the cake board, apply a layer of yellow buttercream, then add a chilled cookie dough disk directly on top of the frosted cake layer. Place another layer of cake on the cookie layer and repeat this process: cake layer, buttercream and cookie dough disk. Place the final cake layer on top of the second cookie dough disk, this time flipping it so the leveled side is facedown.

8. Using your yellow buttercream, crumb coat and final coat your cake, according to the directions on page 34.

(CONTINUED)

DECORATE

9. Return your cake to the turntable, placing a large baking sheet underneath to catch any falling sprinkles. Pour 1 tablespoon (10 g) of sprinkles into your hand at a time and gently apply to the bottom edge of the cake.

10. Refer to page 25 to check whether your ganache has reached the correct consistency for dripping before using. With a teaspoon, drizzle ganache along the top edge of the cake, allowing the drips to run down the sides of the cake. Place the cake in the freezer to allow the ganache to set, about 15 minutes.

11. Pour 1 to 2 tablespoons (12.5 to 25 g) of rainbow nonpareil sprinkles into your hand, then randomly toss them all over the cake, allowing some to fall onto the drips and top also. Place the cake in the freezer to chill for 15 minutes, allowing the drips to set.

12. Using your blue buttercream, pipe eight swirls on top of the cake: Hold your piping bag vertically above the cake, with the tip about ½ inch (1.3 cm) above the surface. Squeeze the bag while moving the tip in a circular motion to form a ring, and without releasing pressure, continue to pipe upward in a spiral. It should taper and come to a point. Gently release pressure as you pull away at the top.

13. Place a maraschino cherry on top of each swirl. Add more sprinkles on top of the cake, if desired.

The cake is freshest if kept in the refrigerator until 1 hour before serving and is best if eaten within 3 days. Add candles before serving (optional).

SPRINKLE SUGAR SKULL

MAKES ONE 6-INCH (15-CM), 4-LAYER ROUND CAKE

SERVES 10 TO 12

Use sprinkles to create an amazing piece of cake art. Sprinkle stencils are a quick and easy way to decorate a cake, but the results are so impressive! In this tutorial, we will use a stencil to create a shape and cover the exposed cake in rainbow nonpareil. Another way to do this is to press sprinkles into the stencil, leaving the rest of the cake exposed. Think: easily recognizable shapes, such as hearts, a tree or a lightning bolt. Here, you will combine Funfetti Cake with a creamy Dulce de Leche filling and Midnight Black Buttercream, all topped off with glittery cherries.

1 batch Dulce de Leche (page 176)

1 batch Funfetti Cake (page 16)

1 batch Midnight Black Buttercream (page 157)

½ batch Simple Vanilla Buttercream (page 18)

Chefmaster pink gel coloring

1 cup (200 g) rainbow nonpareil sprinkles

8 stemmed maraschino cherries, drained

Roxy & Rich black edible glitter

TOOLS

Wilton 1M piping tip

Skull template (printed from my website; more info on page 185)

Parchment paper

X-Acto knife

Large baking sheet

PREP

1. Prepare the Dulce de Leche, Funfetti Cake, making four 6-inch (15-cm) cake layers, and Midnight Black Buttercream.

2. Prepare the Simple Vanilla Buttercream. Place the buttercream in a medium-sized bowl and add 4 to 5 drops of the pink gel coloring. Transfer about 2 cups (600 g) to a piping bag fitted with a 1M tip. This will be used to pipe the buttercream swirls.

ASSEMBLY

3. Fill and stack your cake with the Midnight Black Buttercream and Dulce de Leche, using the dam method as detailed on page 33.

4. Crumb coat and final coat your cake with the Midnight Black Buttercream, according to the directions on page 34.

DECORATE

5. Trace the skull stencil onto a piece of parchment paper. Cut out the skull, using an X-Acto knife. Discard the outer piece, keeping the skull cutout to use on the cake.

6. Once your cake is well chilled, return it to the turntable. Place a large baking sheet underneath to catch any falling sprinkles. Gently attach the skull cutout to the front of the cake; it should stick directly onto the buttercream with very little pressure applied.

(CONTINUED)

SPRINKLE SUGAR SKULL (CONTINUED)

7.   Pour 1 tablespoon (12.5 g) of nonpareil sprinkles into your hand at a time and gently press them onto the surface of the cake. Continue to add sprinkles by hand until the entire surface has been covered, except for the area where the stencil is attached.

8.   Be sure the sprinkles cover the edges of the stencil completely, as well as the inner parts of the skull to ensure a crisp outline. Carefully peel off the stencil. Use a toothpick or cookie scribe to pull up the edges if you are having trouble finding the edge.

9.   Using the pink buttercream, pipe 8 swirls on top of the cake: Hold your piping bag vertically above the cake, with the tip about ½ inch (1.3 cm) above the surface. Squeeze the bag while moving the tip in a circular motion to form a ring, and without releasing pressure, continue to add upward in a spiral. It should taper and come to a point. Gently release pressure as you pull away at the top.

10. Dip the cherries in the black edible glitter and place a glittery cherry on top of each swirl.

The cake is freshest if kept in the refrigerator until 1 hour before serving and is best if eaten within 3 days.

FAIRY DREAMS

MAKES ONE 6-INCH (15-CM), 4-LAYER ROUND CAKE

SERVES 10 TO 12

Pastels, glitter and cotton candy—prepare to be transported to cloud nine! I chose soft and fluffy Classic Vanilla Cake for the layers, accompanied by light Almond Buttercream to complement the delicate designs on the outside. Adding a cotton candy topper is of course optional, but will really give it a big wow factor!

1 batch Classic Vanilla Cake (page 15)

1 batch Almond Buttercream (page 154)

1 cup (200 g) pearlized white nonpareil sprinkles

Wilton Color Mist pink and blue food color sprays

Roxy & Rich pink and blue edible glitters

Store-bought or homemade cotton candy (see Tips)

Purple edible wafer paper butterfly decoration (optional; see Tips)

TOOLS

Large baking sheet

Food-safe paintbrush

PREP

1. Prepare the Classic Vanilla Cake, making four 6-inch (15-cm) cake layers, and the Almond Buttercream.

ASSEMBLY

2. Fill and stack your cake with the Almond Buttercream using the classic method detailed on page 30.

3. Using the Almond Buttercream, crumb coat and final coat your cake, according to the directions on page 34.

DECORATE

4. Return your cake to the turntable and place a large baking sheet underneath to catch any falling sprinkles. Pour 1 tablespoon (12.5 g) of nonpareil sprinkles into your hand at a time and gently press them onto the surface of the cake. Continue to add sprinkles by hand until the entire surface is covered.

5. Begin spraying the cake sparsely with the pink food spray, approximately 12 inches (30 cm) away from the surface of the cake. The goal is to give it a very light dusting of pastel pink. Next, spray blue in any areas where the white is still showing. When the colors overlap, it will create a purple hue, so blend as much or as little as you like.

6. Apply the pink and blue glitter with a food-safe paintbrush, being sure to dust the pink glitter on top of the painted pink areas, and the blue glitter on top of the painted blue areas.

7. Place a large piece of cotton candy directly on top of the cake right before serving, as well as a purple edible butterfly, if using.

The cake is freshest if kept in the refrigerator until 1 hour before serving and is best if eaten within 3 days.

TIPS

- If you have a cotton candy maker at home, try making your own and adding it to the cake for a personal touch. Follow the directions on your machine to make 1 batch. Eat any leftovers for a yummy treat while you wait for your cake to be done!

- Cotton candy melts very quickly and should only be added to the cake right before serving.

- Edible wafer paper butterflies can be found at specialty cake supply stores or on Amazon.

SILVER STARS AT MIDNIGHT

MAKES ONE 6-INCH (15-CM),
4-LAYER ROUND CAKE

SERVES 10 TO 12

This cake combines dramatic colors with a glistening night sky of sprinkles—the embodiment of celestial celebration in cake form. Decadent Chocolate Cake layers filled with a rich Blackberry Filling and creamy Simple Vanilla Buttercream, this cake will leave you feeling starstruck.

4 oz (115 g) packaged white fondant

1 batch Blackberry Filling (page 167)

1 batch Decadent Chocolate Cake (page 139)

1 batch Simple Vanilla Buttercream (page 18)

Roxy & Rich navy powdered coloring plus ½ tsp water to dilute (see Tip)

Wilton gold edible cake paint

¼ cup (52 g) pearlized white nonpareil sprinkles

1 tbsp (10 g) white sugar pearl sprinkles

TOOLS

Moon template (printed from my website; more info on page 185)

Parchment paper

X-Acto knife or scissors

Small, food-safe paintbrush

Large baking sheet

Tweezers (optional)

PREP

1. The moon decoration will need to be prepared ahead of time so it will have a chance to dry before painting. Trace the moon stencil onto a piece of parchment paper. Cut out the moon shape using an X-Acto knife or scissors. Discard the outer piece, keeping the moon cutout. Roll out the fondant to about ⅛ inch (3 mm) in thickness. Place the stencil on the fondant, and using the X-Acto knife, cut out the moon. Set it aside to dry.

2. Prepare the Blackberry Filling and Decadent Chocolate Cake, making four 6-inch (15-cm) cake layers.

3. Prepare the Simple Vanilla Buttercream. In a small bowl, combine 1 teaspoon of the navy powdered coloring and ½ teaspoon of water and stir well. Add the colored paste to the buttercream. Feel free to add more powder to reach a darker shade. Transfer approximately 2 cups (600 g) of the navy-colored buttercream to a piping bag with the end snipped off. This will be used to fill and crumb coat the cake.

4. When the moon cutout is dry, use the paintbrush and gold edible paint to paint the moon gold, then set it aside again to dry.

ASSEMBLY

5. Fill and stack your cake with the navy buttercream and Blackberry Filling using the dam method as detailed on page 33.

6. Crumb coat and final coat your cake with your navy buttercream, according to the directions on page 34.

DECORATE

7. Once the surface of the cake is well chilled, remove from the freezer and place onto the turntable. Place a large baking sheet underneath to catch any falling sprinkles. Pour the nonpareil sprinkles into your hand and apply to the top of the cake, as well as along the top edge. Allow some to trickle down the sides to give them a cascading effect. Add the larger pearls randomly on the top by hand or with tweezers.

8. Once dry, attach the moon to the upper left of the cake. It should stick directly to the buttercream, but if not, attach using a dot of leftover buttercream.

The cake is freshest if kept in the refrigerator until 1 hour before serving and is best if eaten within 3 days.

TIP

- Due to the amount of food coloring needed to achieve the color of navy blue, some staining may occur. Consider adding ½ cup (50 g) of unsweetened cocoa powder and an additional ¼ cup (60 ml) heavy cream to the buttercream when preparing to prevent using as much blue coloring.

ELECTRIC BLUE DRIP

MAKES ONE 6-INCH (15-CM),
4-LAYER ROUND CAKE

SERVES 10 TO 12

*Channel your inner punk and
create a boldly colored drip cake
with attitude! Midnight Black
Buttercream paired with Cookies &
Cream Cake layers, an electric blue
drip and hot pink sprinkles—this
cake is going to rock any party!*

1 batch Cookies & Cream Cake
(page 16)

1 batch Midnight Black Buttercream
(page 157)

1 batch White Chocolate Ganache
Drip (page 24)

Chefmaster turquoise gel coloring

½ cup (95 g) Sprinkle Pop hot pink
sprinkles

8 stemmed maraschino cherries,
drained

Piping gel

Gold edible luster dust

Vodka or food-grade alcohol

TOOLS

Wilton 6B piping tip

Large baking sheet

Food-safe paintbrush

PREP

1. Prepare the Cookies & Cream Cake, making four 6-inch (15-cm) cake layers. Prepare the Midnight Black Buttercream and place 1 to 2 cups (300 to 600 g) in a piping bag fitted with a 6B tip. This will be used to pipe the swirls.

2. Prepare the White Chocolate Ganache Drip. While the ganache is still warm, add 3 drops of turquoise gel coloring. Cover and set aside until ready to use.

ASSEMBLY

3. Fill and stack your cake with the Midnight Black Buttercream, using the classic method as detailed on page 30.

4. Crumb coat and final coat your cake with the Midnight Black Buttercream, according to the directions on page 34.

DECORATE

5. Return your cake to the turntable and place the large baking sheet underneath to catch any falling sprinkles. Pour 1 tablespoon (13 g) of sprinkles into your hand at a time and gently apply to the base of the cake. There will be some left over for dipping the cherries into later.

6. Refer to page 25 to check whether your ganache has reached the correct consistency before using. Pour the ganache on top of the cake, and using the offset spatula, push it toward the edge until it drips off the sides. Place the cake in the freezer to allow the ganache to set, about 15 minutes.

7. Return the cake to the turntable, and using the black buttercream in the piping bag you filled earlier, pipe eight swirls on top: Hold your piping bag vertically above the cake, with the tip about ½ inch (1.3 cm) above the surface. Squeeze the bag while moving the tip in a circular motion to form a ring, and without releasing pressure, continue to pipe upward in a spiral. It should taper and come to a point. Gently release pressure as you pull away at the top.

8. Dip the drained cherries in the piping gel, then into the remaining pink sprinkles. They should stick to the piping gel and coat the cherries completely. Place a sprinkle-coated cherry on top of each swirl.

9. Combine ½ teaspoon of gold luster dust and 1 teaspoon of vodka, mixing until well combined. Using a small paintbrush, splatter the gold mixture all over the cake for a little bit of extra sparkle.

The cake is freshest if kept in the refrigerator until 1 hour before serving and is best if eaten within 3 days.

TREAT YO'SELF

TOTALLY DOABLE CANDY-THEMED CAKES!

Ever met someone who didn't like candy? Okay, maybe a few sad individuals, but most people's eyes light up at the sight of brightly colored gumballs and swirly lollipops. Using candy elements on a cake is a fun way to add color and texture, while also creating a unique three-dimensional effect. Candy cakes are especially popular for children's birthday parties, but these will appeal to the inner child in all of us!

QUEEN OF HEARTS

MAKES ONE 6-INCH (15-CM), 4-LAYER ROUND CAKE

SERVES 10 TO 12

Inspired by the Queen of Hearts herself, this cake is unique, delicious and quirky all at once. Red is normally a color most cake decorators shy away from because of the sheer amount of food coloring required. I use a powdered red coloring, which works far better and makes it much easier to achieve a true red than when using gel food coloring. Cherry Swirl Cake layers with Cheesecake Filling and creamy Simple Vanilla Buttercream, it is sure to become a fanciful favorite.

1 batch Cherry Swirl Cake (page 16)

1 batch Cheesecake Filling (page 175)

1½ batches Simple Vanilla Buttercream (page 18)

Roxy & Rich super red powdered coloring plus ½ tsp water to dilute

3 graham crackers, crushed into crumbs

Bakery Bling Drenched in Diamonds glittery sugar

10 to 12 red foil–wrapped heart-shaped chocolates

8 stemmed maraschino cherries, drained

TOOLS

Wilton 2D and 8B piping tips

Large baking sheet

Cookie scribe or toothpick

PREP

1. Prepare the Cherry Swirl Cake, making four 6-inch (15-cm) cake layers. Prepare the Cheesecake Filling, place it in a piping bag whose end has been snipped off and set aside.

2. Prepare the Simple Vanilla Buttercream. Transfer 1 cup (300 g) to a piping bag fitted with a Wilton 2D tip and a second cup (300 g) to a piping bag fitted with a Wilton 8B tip. These will be used to pipe the borders.

3. In a small bowl, combine 1 teaspoon of super red powdered coloring with ½ teaspoon of water and stir well. Add the diluted color paste to the remaining buttercream. Place 1 cup (300 g) of the red-colored buttercream in a piping bag with the end snipped off. This will be used to fill the cake.

ASSEMBLY

4. Fill and stack your cake with the Cheesecake Filling and red-colored Simple Vanilla Buttercream using the dam method as detailed on page 33. Sprinkle the graham cracker crumbs on top of the Cheesecake Filling on each layer.

5. Crumb coat and final coat your cake with the remaining red-colored Simple Vanilla Buttercream, according to the directions on page 34.

DECORATE

6. Return the cake to the turntable and place the large baking sheet underneath to catch any falling sugar. Pour the glittery sugar into the palm of your hand and, pressing gently, glide your hand up the cake to coat the surface. Cover the entire surface in this manner, including the top.

7. Keeping them in their foil wrappers, press the heart-shaped chocolates into the cake in two rows, offsetting each one in a zigzag pattern. If they are not sticking, pipe a dot of leftover buttercream onto the back first.

8. Using the uncolored buttercream in the 8B tip–fitted piping bag, pipe 8 dots on top of the cake: Hold your piping bag vertically above the cake, with the tip about ½ inch (1.3 cm) above the surface. Squeeze the bag to create a large star shape, releasing pressure as you pull away at the top.

9. Using the uncolored buttercream in the 2D tip–fitted piping bag, pipe a shell border along the bottom edge: Hold the bag at an angle with the tip pointing away from you, parallel to the cake. Squeeze the bag as you flick your wrist upward and outward to form a closed C shape. Pipe these loops in a continuous border running lengthwise, each loop slightly overlapping the tail of the previous loop. End the border when you return to where you began piping.

10. Place a maraschino cherry on top of each piped star.

The cake is freshest if kept in the refrigerator until 1 hour before serving and is best if eaten within 3 days.

LADY LICORICE

MAKES ONE 6-INCH (15-CM), 4-LAYER ROUND CAKE

SERVES 10 TO 12

Inspired by a nostalgic childhood candy you may only know about if you lived in the UK, Australia, New Zealand or Canada, this cake incorporates all the flavors and colors of the unique candy known as Licorice Allsorts, while giving it an edgy, modern twist. If you've never had the chance to try it, you are in for a literal treat! Toasted Coconut Cake layers complement the taste of the candy, while the licorice-like flavor of the Anise Buttercream echoes it.

1 batch Toasted Coconut Cake batter (unbaked) (page 16)

Chefmaster pink, bright green, lemon yellow, sunset orange, coal black and sky blue gel coloring

1 batch Dark Chocolate Ganache Frosting (page 163)

1 batch Anise Buttercream (page 20)

1 batch Dark Chocolate Ganache Drip (page 23)

1 (7-oz [200-g]) bag Licorice Allsorts candy

PREP

1. Prepare the Toasted Coconut Cake batter and prepare your four 6-inch (15-cm) cake pans according to the directions on page 12. Divide the batter evenly among four small bowls. Add 5 drops of pink gel coloring to the first bowl, 5 drops of bright green gel to the second, 5 drops of lemon yellow gel to the third and 5 drops of sunset orange gel to the fourth bowl, stirring each bowl well to incorporate the color.

2. Pour each colored bowlful of batter into a separate prepared pan and bake your cakes according to the directions on page 15.

3. Prepare the Dark Chocolate Ganache Frosting. While the ganache is still warm, add 5 drops of coal black gel coloring. Stir gently until the color is well incorporated. Cover and set aside until the ganache has cooled.

4. Prepare the Anise Buttercream and add 5 drops of sky blue gel coloring.

5. Prepare the Dark Chocolate Ganache Drip. While the ganache is still warm, add 5 drops of coal black gel coloring. Cover and set aside until ready to use.

ASSEMBLY

6. Fill and stack your cake with the Black Chocolate Ganache Frosting using the classic method as described on page 30. Stack the colors in any order you like! I used pink at the bottom, followed by yellow, then green and finally orange at the top.

7. Crumb coat and final coat your cake with the colored Anise Buttercream, according to the directions on page 34.

DECORATE

8. Return the cake to the turntable once it has chilled, referring to page 25 to check whether your ganache drip has reached the correct consistency for dripping. Pour the ganache drip on top of the cake and, using an offset spatula, push it toward the edge until it drips off the sides. Place the cake in the freezer to allow the ganache to set, about 15 minutes.

9. Return the cake to the turntable and pile the candy on top of the cake.

The cake is freshest if kept in the refrigerator until 1 hour before serving and is best if eaten within 3 days.

I SPY ORANGE

MAKES ONE 6-INCH (15-CM), 4-LAYER ROUND CAKE

SERVES 10 TO 12

While I was growing up in the '90s, I Spy books were all the rage, and this cake clearly took inspiration from the massively popular concept. The idea was a page filled to the brim with beautifully curated items of a similar theme and you were required to find certain pieces within it. In this case, spot the jelly bean or the M&M! This cake is made up of moist Orange Dreamsicle Cake layers, has a White Chocolate Ganache Filling and is all wrapped up in a tangy Orange Sherbet Buttercream.

1 batch Orange Dreamsicle Cake (page 140)

1 batch White Chocolate Ganache Frosting (page 160)

1 batch Orange Sherbet Buttercream (page 20)

Chefmaster sunset orange gel coloring

Assortment of orange-colored candy: lollipops, sugared orange slices, butterscotch, fruit chews, Spree, candy corn, candy pumpkins, jelly beans, gumballs, M&M's, caramel popcorn, Reese's Pieces

6 orange cream–filled chocolate sandwich cookies, such as Oreos

TOOLS

Wilton 1M piping tip

PREP

1. Prepare the Orange Dreamsicle Cake, making four 6-inch (15-cm) cake layers. Prepare the White Chocolate Ganache Frosting, then cover and set aside to cool.

2. Prepare the Orange Sherbet Buttercream. Add 4 to 6 drops of sunset orange gel coloring. Transfer 1 cup (300 g) of the colored buttercream to a small bowl and add an additional 3 to 4 drops of sunset orange gel to it for a deeper shade. Place the darker buttercream in a piping bag fitted with a 1M tip. This will be used to pipe the swirls on top.

ASSEMBLY

3. Fill and stack your cake with White Chocolate Ganache Frosting using the classic method as detailed on page 30. Crumb coat and final coat your cake with the lighter colored Orange Sherbet Buttercream, according to the directions on page 34.

DECORATE

4. Return the cake to the turntable and press the orange candies onto the sides of the cake in rows. If you are having a difficult time attaching the candy, pipe a dot of leftover buttercream onto the back of each before pressing onto the cake. Cover the entire surface in rows of candy, alternating between the different varieties.

5. Arrange the six cookies around the top edge of the cake, spacing them out equally. Using the piping bag of darker orange buttercream, pipe a swirl in between each cookie: Hold your piping bag vertically above the cake, with the tip resting just above the surface. Squeeze the bag while moving the tip in a circular motion to form a ring and without releasing pressure, continue to pipe upward in a spiral. It should taper and come to a point. Gently release pressure as you pull away at the top. Pipe eight swirls in total.

The cake is freshest if kept in the refrigerator until 1 hour before serving and is best if eaten within 3 days.

DOUBLE BUBBLE

MAKES ONE 6-INCH (15-CM), 4-LAYER ROUND CAKE

SERVES 10 TO 12

Funnily enough, it's usually the sweet and simple cake designs that stir up the most excitement within my cake community! This playful bubblegum baby is no exception and combines the classic flavor of bubblegum in both the layers and buttercream with bright, popping colors for a complete party in your mouth!

1 batch Bubblegum Cake (page 16)

1 batch Bubblegum Buttercream (page 20)

Chefmaster pink gel coloring

12 to 15 regular-sized gumballs in assorted colors

10 to 12 mini gumballs in assorted colors

TOOLS

Scissors

PREP

1. Prepare the Bubblegum Cake, making four 6-inch (15-cm) cake layers. Prepare the Bubblegum Buttercream and add 10 drops of pink gel coloring.

ASSEMBLY

2. Fill and stack your cake with the Bubblegum Buttercream using the classic method as detailed on page 30.

3. Crumb coat and final coat your cake with the Bubblegum Buttercream, according to the directions on page 34.

DECORATE

4. To prepare the gumballs, carefully cut each regular-sized gumball in half using a pair of sharp scissors or a knife. (Make sure to be cautious while doing this, and please have an adult help with this step for younger bakers.)

5. Return the cake to the turntable, and randomly place the halved gumballs, domed side out, on all sides of the cake. Place the smaller gumballs in the spaces in between the larger ones.

The cake is freshest if kept in the refrigerator until 1 hour before serving and is best if eaten within 3 days.

TIP

- You could cut a circle from the middle of each cake layer and frost as normal, adding candy, gumballs or even sprinkles to the cavity. When cut open, the candy will spill out and surprise everyone!

SEEING STRIPES

BRILLIANT BUTTERCREAM COLOR COMBOS

Ready to impress your friends? You've crushed the basics; now it's time to up the ante. This technique is not as difficult as it appears, and after you've learned a few simple tricks, it may become one of your favorites!

Buttercream stripes are a fun and simple way to express a theme. Think: red and green for the holidays, black and gold for graduation or even the colors of your favorite sports team—and don't think you have to stop at just two colors! Stripes are my go-to when I'm short on time and is a technique I'd recommend every cake designer add to their repertoire.

OVER THE RAINBOW

This cake will be sure to put you, and everyone else who sees it, in a bright and happy mood! I wanted to create something a little different than your typical rainbow cake, and that's where the black stripes come into play. Black always brings out other colors in a big way, and when you use all the colors of the rainbow, it creates quite the wow factor! This is a Decadent Chocolate Cake coated in a delicious Baileys-infused buttercream with a White Chocolate Ganache Drip.

1 batch Decadent Chocolate Cake (page 139)

1 batch Midnight Black Buttercream (page 157)

1 batch Baileys Buttercream (page 20)

Chefmaster bright pink, bright purple, bright blue, bright green, bright yellow and bright orange gel coloring

1 batch White Chocolate Ganache Drip (page 24)

¼ cup (40 g) Sprinkle Pop "Rainbow Beam" sprinkles (optional)

TOOLS

Wilton 1A and 8B piping tips

8 to 10 piping bags

Cake scraping comb (with evenly spaced grooves)

Plastic wrap

PREP

1. Prepare the Decadent Chocolate Cake, making four 6-inch (15-cm) cake layers, the Midnight Black Buttercream and Baileys Buttercream.

2. Divide the Baileys Buttercream among six bowls, placing 2¾ cups (825 g) in one bowl and ¾ cup (225 g) in each of the remaining five bowls. There should be a small amount of buttercream remaining, approximately ½ cup (150 g). Transfer this uncolored buttercream to a piping bag fitted with the 1A tip. This will be used to pipe the clouds.

3. To the 2¾ cups (825 g) of buttercream, add 8 to 10 drops of pink gel coloring. Add 5 drops of purple gel to the second bowl, 5 drops of blue gel to the third bowl, 5 drops of green gel to the fourth bowl, 5 drops of yellow gel to the fifth bowl and 5 drops of orange gel to the sixth bowl.

4. Scoop ¾ cup (225 g) of pink buttercream into a piping bag, and snip about 1 inch (2.5 cm) off the end. Scoop each of the other colors into individual piping bags and snip off the ends similarly. These colors will be used to fill in the rainbow stripes.

ASSEMBLY

5. Fill and stack your cake with the pink buttercream using the classic method as detailed on page 30.

6. Crumb coat and final coat your cake with the Midnight Black Buttercream, according to the directions on page 34.

DECORATE

7. Return the cake to the turntable. Hold the icing comb at a 45-degree angle to the cake and begin to gently scrape all the way around. Try to avoid digging in too much; we are just taking off a little bit at a time.

8. Remove any buttercream that builds up on the comb, and wipe with a cloth before continuing to scrape. We do not want to get any of the excess buttercream back onto the cake. It will take some time and look quite messy before you see any deep grooves, but have patience and continue to scrape. Fill in any of the stripes that look incomplete with a little bit of extra Midnight Black Buttercream and continue to scrape. The cleaner your grooves, the crisper the stripes will be. Once the stripes have formed, return the cake to the freezer to chill for about 15 minutes before adding the other colors. This will help prevent the colors from mixing with the base layer.

(CONTINUED)

9. Return the cake to the turntable and pipe the purple buttercream into the groove at the very bottom. Be sure to fill the groove completely, without leaving any gaps. Pipe the blue buttercream into the second groove, green into the third groove, yellow into the fourth groove, orange into the fifth groove and pink into the sixth groove.

10. With your tall bench scraper, scrape all the excess buttercream off the cake. Be sure to clean the scraper in between swipes to avoid transferring buttercream back onto the stripes. Avoid pressing too firmly while scraping; we are only removing the excess buttercream on the surface to reveal the stripes underneath. If you see any holes or gaps, apply a small amount of buttercream in the corresponding color to the area. Continue to scrape until clean stripes appear. If you overscrape, you could risk revealing the crumb-coated layer underneath. To achieve a sharp top edge, chill the cake for a few minutes and slice off the buttercream that has built up at the top. Alternatively, pull the buttercream around the top edge into the center using an offset spatula. Remove any excess. Place the cake back in the freezer to chill for about 15 minutes.

11. While the cake is chilling, prepare the White Chocolate Ganache Drip and set aside to reach room temperature.

12. Lay down a piece of plastic wrap about 16 inches (40 cm) long, and pipe a line lengthwise with the remaining yellow, orange and pink buttercream. Fold the plastic wrap widthwise to form a thick tube, twisting the ends to secure. Snip about 1 inch (2.5 cm) off one end. Place the tube of buttercream in a piping bag fitted with the 8B tip. This will be used to pipe the border on top.

13. Return the cake to the turntable. Refer to page 25 to check whether your White Chocolate Ganache Drip has reached the correct consistency. Using a teaspoon, drizzle the ganache along the top edge of the cake as well as in the center to cover the top. Alternate the amount of ganache you add to each drip to achieve varied lengths.

14. Using the uncolored buttercream, pipe small clouds along the bottom edge of the cake. These shapes should look irregular and have clusters of five to eight dots. To achieve a dot instead of a point, flick your wrist in a circular motion while releasing pressure as you pull away.

15. Using the 8B-fitted piping bag, pipe a rope border along the top edge. Hold your bag at a 45-degree angle to the top of the cake. Facing to the right (or to the left if you are left-handed), touch the tip to the surface of the cake and, using even pressure, begin piping small spirals along the edge. Be sure these spirals lay against each other and form tight loops. If you need to allow your hand a break, stop looping on the inside, readjust and continue the same loop. These loops should look just like old phone cords, and loop in the same direction around the entire edge. When you reach where you started, tuck the end under the loop you began with. Try to rotate the cake instead of moving your piping bag; this will help you achieve evenly sized loops.

16. Add rainbow sprinkles to the top of the cake, if desired.

The cake is freshest if kept in the refrigerator until 1 hour before serving and is best if eaten within 3 days.

NEON LEOPARD PRINT

MAKES ONE 6-INCH (15-CM),
4-LAYER ROUND CAKE

SERVES 10 TO 12

What do you get if you cross a rainbow with leopard spots? Well, I'm not sure exactly, but this cake was heavily inspired by the work of popular '90s artist Lisa Frank. The techniques you'll learn in this tutorial are multifaceted and combine simple stripes and stencil work for a showstopping design. Prepare to have fun and probably make a bit of a mess with this groovy party cake.

1 batch Classic Vanilla Cake batter
(unbaked) (page 15)

Chefmaster pink, sunset orange, lemon yellow, bright green, violet and sky blue gel coloring

1 batch Simple Vanilla Buttercream
(page 18)

½ batch Midnight Black Buttercream
(page 157)

TOOLS

Toothpick or cookie scribe

7 piping bags

Sweet Stamp leopard spot cake stencil

4 T pins

Rainbow balloon cake topper kit
(I found mine in the party supplies section at Walmart.)

PREP

1. Prepare the Classic Vanilla Cake batter and prepare your cake pans according to the directions on page 12. Divide the batter equally among five medium-sized bowls. Add 5 drops of Chefmaster pink gel to the first bowl, 5 drops of sunset orange gel to the second bowl, 5 drops of lemon yellow gel to the third bowl, 5 drops of bright green gel to the fourth bowl and 5 drops of violet gel to the fifth bowl. Stir each until the colors are well incorporated.

2. Scoop spoonfuls from each bowl into the prepared pans, alternating among the colors. Using a toothpick, gently swirl the colors together. Bake according to the directions on page 15.

3. Prepare the Simple Vanilla Buttercream. Prepare the Midnight Black Buttercream and set aside; this will be used to create the stenciled spots.

ASSEMBLY

4. Fill and stack your cake with the Simple Vanilla Buttercream using the classic method as detailed on page 30.

5. Crumb coat your cake using the Simple Vanilla Buttercream, according to the directions on page 34.

6. Divide the remaining Simple Vanilla Buttercream among six bowls, about ½ cup (150 g) per bowl. Add 10 drops of pink gel coloring to the first bowl, 15 drops of sunset orange gel to the second bowl, 10 drops of lemon yellow gel to the third bowl, 5 drops of sky blue gel to the fourth bowl, 6 drops of bright green gel to the fifth bowl and 8 drops of violet gel to the sixth bowl. Still reserving the Midnight Black Buttercream, place each colored buttercream in a separate piping bag and snip about 1 inch (2.5 cm) off the end. These colors will be used to create the rainbow stripes.

DECORATE

7. Return the cake to the turntable. Using the blue buttercream, pipe two rings around the bottom edge of the cake.

8. Next, directly above the blue rings of buttercream, pipe two rings of green buttercream, followed by two rings of yellow buttercream, then two rings of orange buttercream, two rings of pink buttercream and finally two rings of violet buttercream.

(CONTINUED)

NEON LEOPARD PRINT (CONTINUED)

9. Pipe the violet buttercream onto the very top of the cake and, using your offset spatula, scrape to smooth and level the top. Holding the tall bench scraper at a 45-degree angle to the cake, gently smooth around the entire cake. The goal is to remove only the surface layer, so try not to remove too much buttercream at a time.

10. Scrape any excess buttercream from the bench scraper and wipe with a clean cloth. This will keep the colors clean and prevent the stripes from blending on the cake. Fill in any gaps with the remaining buttercream in the piping bags and continue to scrape until the surface is completely smooth and level. Place the frosted cake in the freezer to chill for approximately 20 minutes, or in the refrigerator for 3 to 4 hours.

11. Return the chilled cake to the turntable and attach the leopard print stencil to the cake using the T pins to secure it. Once the stencil has been secured, apply the Midnight Black Buttercream using the offset spatula. Scrape any excess with the bench scraper.

12. Be sure to rinse and dry the stencil in between applications to prevent any unwanted smearing or smudging. Continue adding panels (two or three in total) until the entire cake is covered in spots. It is important to be gentle during this process, as you do not want to damage the buttercream underneath. Also, if your cake has any condensation on the surface, it will cause the stencil to stick to the buttercream underneath and you will not be able to achieve a clean transfer. To fill in the small space between the stencils (depending on how large your stencil is), chill the cake in the freezer for approximately 20 minutes before pinning the clean stencil to the area without stenciled spots. Apply buttercream to only this area and gently peel it away from the cake.

13. Prepare the rainbow balloon topper and place it on top of the cake as a finishing touch.

The cake is freshest if kept in the refrigerator until 1 hour before serving and is best if eaten within 3 days.

VINTAGE CANDY STRIPE

MAKES ONE 6-INCH (15-CM), 4-LAYER ROUND CAKE

SERVES 10 TO 12

Peppermint, stripes and everything nice—if you weren't in the mood for some holiday cheer, you will be now! This cake not only looks like a peppermint stick on the outside, but it is filled with lots of pepperminty goodness on the inside to match! Add a touch of sparkle and fluffy buttercream borders for the complete holiday package.

1 batch Peppermint Cake (page 16)

1 batch Peppermint Buttercream (page 20; see Tips)

Roxy & Rich super red powdered coloring plus ½ tsp water to dilute (see Tips)

Chefmaster pink gel coloring

1 batch Dark Chocolate Ganache Frosting (page 163; see Tips)

8 maraschino cherries

Roxy & Rich red edible glitter

Bakery Bling Drenched in Diamonds glittery sugar (optional)

20 to 22 round peppermint candies

TOOLS

4 piping bags

Candy stripe comb

Wilton 1M piping tip

PREP

1. Prepare the Peppermint Cake, making four 6-inch (15-cm) cake layers, and the Peppermint Buttercream.

2. Place ¼ teaspoon powdered red coloring in a small bowl and combine with ½ teaspoon of water, mixing until no lumps remain. In two bowls, place 1 cup (300 g) of buttercream into each and add 2 to 3 drops of pink gel coloring to the first bowl, and the diluted red color to the second bowl. Transfer the red and pink buttercream into two separate piping bags and snip about 1 inch (2.5 cm) off the ends.

3. Prepare the Dark Chocolate Ganache Frosting. Once set, transfer to a piping bag with the end snipped off. This will be used to fill the cake.

ASSEMBLY

4. Fill and stack your cake with the Dark Chocolate Ganache Frosting using the classic method as detailed on page 30.

5. Crumb coat and final coat your cake with the remaining uncolored Peppermint Buttercream, according to the directions on page 34.

DECORATE

6. Return your cake to the turntable. Holding the candy stripe comb at a 45-degree angle to the cake, begin gently scraping all the way around. Try to avoid digging in too much; we are just taking off a little bit at a time.

7. Remove any buttercream that builds up on the comb, and wipe with a cloth before continuing to scrape. We do not want to get any of the excess buttercream back onto the cake. It will take some time and look quite messy before you see any deep grooves, but have patience and continue to scrape. Fill in any of the stripes that look incomplete with a little bit of extra uncolored buttercream and continue to scrape. The cleaner your grooves, the crisper the stripes will be. Once the stripes have formed, return the cake to the freezer to chill for about 15 minutes before adding the other colors. This will help prevent the colors from mixing with the base layer.

(CONTINUED)

8. Once chilled, return the cake to the turntable. Pipe red buttercream into the wider grooves and pink buttercream into the narrower grooves. Be sure to fill the grooves completely, without leaving any gaps.

9. With the tall bench scraper, scrape all the excess buttercream off the cake. Be sure to clean the scraper in between swipes to avoid transferring buttercream back onto the stripes. Avoid pressing too firmly while scraping; we are only removing the excess buttercream on the surface to reveal stripes underneath. If you see any holes or gaps, apply a small amount of buttercream in the corresponding color to the area. Continue to scrape until clean stripes appear. If you overscrape, you could risk revealing the crumb-coated layer underneath.

10. To achieve a sharp top edge, chill the cake for a few minutes and slice off the buttercream that has built up at the top.

11. Attach the 1M tip to the piping bag with the remaining pink buttercream. Pipe eight swirls on top of the cake: Hold your piping bag vertically above the cake, with the tip resting just above the surface. Squeeze the bag while moving the tip in a circular motion to form a ring, and without releasing pressure, continue to pipe upward in a spiral. It should taper and come to a point. Gently release pressure as you pull away at the top.

12. Dip the cherries in the red glitter, placing a glittery cherry on top of each swirl. Sprinkle the top of the cake with the glittery sugar, if desired.

13. Press the round peppermint candies along the bottom edge side by side, wrapping around the entire cake.

The cake is freshest if kept in the refrigerator until 1 hour before serving and is best if eaten within 3 days.

TIPS

- Instead of adding extra red coloring to deepen the shade (this often makes the buttercream bitter and will stain your mouth), it is best to prepare the red buttercream a few hours ahead of time and allow the color to mature. The longer it sits the darker it will become.

- For an extra minty flavor, add 1 teaspoon of peppermint extract to the Dark Chocolate Ganache Frosting after it has cooled to room temperature.

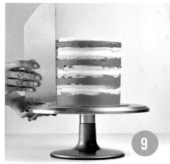

PRETTY IN PINK OMBRÉ

MAKES ONE 6-INCH (15-CM), 4-LAYER ROUND CAKE

SERVES 10 TO 12

Ombré cakes are always a popular option and can be created using any color to match any occasion. They are very simple in technique and can be whipped up in no time at all. Add some seasonal decorations, such as fresh flowers and berries, on top for a touch of sophistication. This cake combines moist red velvet layers with tangy Cream Cheese Frosting for a melt-in-your-mouth experience.

1 batch Red Velvet Cake (page 143)

1 batch Cream Cheese Frosting (page 164)

Chefmaster pink gel coloring

Assortment of fuchsia and pink flowers (orchids, roses, carnations)

1 to 3 fresh strawberries

TOOLS

4 piping bags

Floral tape

PREP

1. Prepare the Red Velvet Cake, making four 6-inch (15-cm) cake layers, and the Cream Cheese Frosting.

ASSEMBLY

2. Fill and stack your cake with the Cream Cheese Frosting using the classic method as detailed on page 30.

3. Crumb coat your cake using the Cream Cheese Frosting, according to the directions on page 34.

4. Divide the remaining Cream Cheese Frosting equally among three bowls. Add 12 drops of pink gel coloring to the first bowl, 8 drops to the second bowl and 3 drops to the third bowl. Transfer the buttercream from each bowl into three individual piping bags, and snip about 1 inch (2.5 cm) off the ends.

DECORATE

5. Return the cake to the turntable, and pipe four rings of the darkest pink frosting onto the base of the cake, followed by four rings of the medium pink frosting to the middle section of the cake, and finally, four rings of the light pink frosting to the top of the cake.

6. Scrape the cake, using the tall bench scraper, until you have a smooth surface. You may have to add a little bit of extra frosting if there are uneven spaces. Blend the buttercream in the areas where the colors meet using your offset spatula for a softer color gradient. Place the cake in the freezer to chill while you prepare your other decorations.

7. Cut the stems of each flower 2 inches (5 cm) from the blossom. Wrap the stems in floral tape to protect the cake from coming in direct contact with the flowers.

8. Arrange the flowers and strawberries on top of the cake, inserting the wrapped stems into the top. It may take some creativity in finding the correct placement, but use the photo as a guide to achieve a good balance.

The cake is freshest if kept in the refrigerator until 1 hour before serving and is best if eaten within 3 days.

PRETTY PIPING

MASTER CUTE AND CONTEMPORARY PIPED DESIGNS

Learning how to utilize piping techniques is going to completely change the game! With just a handful of tips, you can create borders, flowers, grass, patterns, transfers and so many other things! Most of the techniques you'll learn in this chapter not only apply to cakes, but are also used in a variety of decorations on cupcakes and cookies as well. Whether you're creating a dainty flower, an intricate pattern or a fluffy border, buttercream piping is going to be a foundational technique you will use on almost every cake.

STRAW-BERRY PATCH

MAKES ONE 6-INCH (15-CM), 4-LAYER ROUND CAKE

SERVES 10 TO 12

I remember flipping through old Wilton magazines as a kid and seeing all the novelty cakes frosted with this piping technique. Using buttercream "stars" to cover areas or create patterns and shapes is an amazing technique to learn, and it is quite simple to do while creating a beautifully intricate effect. This is a moist strawberry layer cake with fresh Strawberry Filling and creamy Vanilla Buttercream, decorated in cutesy piped strawberries.

1 batch Strawberry Filling (page 167)

1 batch Pink Strawberry Cake (page 16)

1 batch Simple Vanilla Buttercream (page 18)

Roxy & Rich super red powdered coloring plus ½ tsp water to dilute (see Tip)

Chefmaster leaf green and pink gel coloring

White sprinkles

TOOLS

4 piping bags

2 Wilton no. 16 piping tips

Strawberry-shaped cookie cutter

PREP

1. Prepare the Strawberry Filling. Once set, transfer to a piping bag with the end snipped off. This will be used to fill the cake. Prepare the Pink Strawberry Cake, making four 6-inch (15-cm) cake layers, and the Simple Vanilla Buttercream.

2. Place ¼ teaspoon of powdered red coloring in a small bowl and combine with ½ teaspoon of water, mixing until no lumps remain.

3. Place 1 cup (300 g) of the buttercream in a small bowl and add the diluted red coloring. Place ½ cup (150 g) of uncolored buttercream in a second small bowl and add 2 to 3 drops of leaf green gel coloring. Transfer both the red and the green buttercream to separate piping bags, each fitted with a no. 16 tip. These colors will be used to pipe the strawberries. To the remaining uncolored buttercream in your stand mixer bowl, add 3 to 4 drops of pink gel.

ASSEMBLY

4. Fill and stack your cake with the pink buttercream and Strawberry Filling using the dam method as detailed on page 33.

5. Crumb coat and final coat your cake using the pink buttercream, according to the directions on page 34.

DECORATE

6. Return the cake to the turntable and gently press the strawberry-shaped cookie cutter into the surface of the buttercream to create an outline. The strawberries should be approximately 1 inch (2.5 cm) apart and cover the entire cake.

7. Pipe an outline of green to form the leaf and fill in the area in the center. Use short bursts while piping, squeezing to release a small amount of buttercream against the cake and then pulling away to form a star. Avoid squeezing as you pull away.

8. Using the red buttercream, pipe along the outline of the body of the strawberry, working inward and filling the center as well. Fill in all the strawberries and leaves on the cake.

9. Once they have all been piped, add 7 or 8 white sprinkles to each berry to resemble the seeds.

The cake is freshest if kept in the refrigerator until 1 hour before serving and is best if eaten within 3 days.

TIP

• Instead of adding extra red coloring to deepen the shade (this often makes the buttercream bitter and will stain your mouth), it is best to prepare the red buttercream a few hours ahead of time and allow the color to mature. The longer it sits the darker it will become.

PEARLS AND DIAMONDS

MAKES ONE 6-INCH (15-CM), 4-LAYER ROUND CAKE

SERVES 10 TO 12

Monochrome cakes are one of my favorite styles and rely more on texture and detail than bright color. This light vanilla cake with lemon filling and fluffy Italian Meringue Buttercream is decorated with delicate piped florals and ivory pearls. This elegant cake would be perfect for a simple wedding or bridal shower and could be made in any size. Piping buttercream flowers doesn't always have to be difficult and time consuming—learning how to pipe them directly onto the cake may just become your new favorite technique.

1 batch Lemon Curd (page 172)

1 batch Classic Vanilla Cake (page 15)

1 batch Italian Meringue Buttercream (page 152)

White sprinkles in varied sizes and shades (beads, pearls, nonpareil, sixlets)

Silver sprinkles in varied sizes (dragees, balls, beads)

TOOLS
4 piping bags

Wilton no. 97 and 97L piping tips

PREP

1. Prepare the Lemon Curd. Once set, transfer to a piping bag with the end snipped off. This will be used to fill the cake. Prepare the Classic Vanilla Cake, making four 6-inch (15-cm) cake layers.

2. Prepare the Italian Meringue Buttercream and transfer 1 cup (300 g) to a piping bag with the end snipped off. This will be used along with the Lemon Curd to fill the cake.

ASSEMBLY

3. Fill and stack your cake with the Italian Meringue Buttercream and Lemon Curd using the dam method on page 33.

4. Crumb coat and final coat your cake with the Italian Meringue Buttercream, according to the directions on page 34.

5. Place ½ cup (150 g) of buttercream in a piping bag fitted with the 97 tip and ½ cup (150 g) in a piping bag fitted with the 97L tip. These will be used to pipe the flower petals.

DECORATE

6. Return the cake to the turntable once it is well chilled. Start with the 97L piping tip and position it near the upper left edge. With the tip flat against the surface of the cake, and the narrow end pointed away from you, squeeze and pull in a small semicircle to form a petal. Your tip should end in the same place it began. Allow the buttercream to ruffle slightly by applying more pressure as you pipe to give it a more natural appearance.

7. Pipe the second petal in the same manner, beginning in the same place in the center and piping directly beside the first petal.

8. Pipe four or five individual petals to form a flower. Alternating between the 97L and the 97 tips, pipe flowers in a crescent layout along the top edge. The flowers can have anywhere from three to six petals per blossom; simply aim to balance the layout by creating a variety of different sizes and shapes. Allow some of the flowers to cascade down the front of the cake diagonally from the crescent.

9. Pipe a cluster of flowers in the bottom right corner, diagonal to the ending point of the crescent shape on top.

10. With the 97 tip, pipe single petals in between a few of the flowers to fill any large spaces. Add a few cascading down from the top to look like falling petals.

11. Using the largest beads or sprinkles, place them in between the flowers and petals. Place 3 or 4 small sugar pearls in the center of each flower to form the pistils and stamens. Sprinkle the smaller beads (both white and silver) between the flowers along the crescent and at the bottom. Allow some sprinkles to fall randomly to add texture and dimension to the cake.

The cake is freshest if kept in the refrigerator until 1 hour before serving and is best if eaten within 3 days.

ENGLISH GARDEN ROSE

MAKES ONE 6-INCH (15-CM), 4-LAYER ROUND CAKE

SERVES 10 TO 12

Pointillism is a new trend in cake decorating, made hugely popular by cake decorating extraordinaire Sian-Amy Pettit. This technique is incredibly time consuming and tedious, but creates an exceptional edible design rivaled by none other. Be forewarned, this design takes some serious patience and wrist strength, but the payoff is unparalleled. This cake is not only beautiful on the outside, but delicious on the inside with Decadent Chocolate Cake layers and a dark chocolate ganache filling, with a slight hint of raspberry.

1 batch Raspberry Filling (page 167)

1 batch Decadent Chocolate Cake (page 139)

1 batch Simple Vanilla Buttercream (page 18)

½ batch Midnight Black Buttercream (page 157; see Tips)

2 batches Dark Chocolate Ganache Frosting (page 163)

Roxy & Rich super red powdered coloring plus ½ tsp water to dilute (see Tips)

Chefmaster pink, lemon yellow and turquoise gel coloring

TOOLS

5 piping bags

4 Wilton no. 3 piping tips

Cookie scribe or toothpick

PREP

1. Prepare the Raspberry Filling, Decadent Chocolate Cake, making four 6-inch (15-cm) cake layers, and Simple Vanilla Buttercream.

2. Prepare the Midnight Black Buttercream and transfer 1 cup (300 g) to a piping bag fitted with a no. 3 tip.

3. Prepare the Dark Chocolate Ganache Frosting and transfer to a piping bag with the end snipped off. This will be used to fill and crumb coat the cake.

4. Place ¼ teaspoon powdered red coloring in a small bowl and combine with ½ teaspoon of water, mixing until no lumps remain.

5. Place 1 cup (300 g) of Simple Vanilla Buttercream in a bowl and add 2 drops of pink gel coloring and 1 drop of lemon yellow gel. Place ½ cup (150 g) of uncolored buttercream in a second bowl and add the diluted red coloring. Place ½ cup (150 g) of uncolored buttercream in a third bowl and add 2 or 3 drops of the turquoise gel. Transfer each color to a separate piping bag fitted with a no. 3 tip. These will be used to pipe the designs.

ASSEMBLY

6. Using the classic method detailed on page 30, fill and stack your cake with the Dark Chocolate Ganache Frosting, spreading 1 to 2 tablespoons (20 to 40 g) of the Raspberry Filling between each layer on top of the ganache for extra flavor.

7. Crumb coat your cake using the Dark Chocolate Ganache Frosting, according to the directions on page 34.

DECORATE

8. Return the cake to the turntable once the surface is completely chilled. Using the cookie scribe, sketch the roses and leaves into the ganache-coated cake (more in-depth directions about creating these shapes follow). These markings will help guide where to pipe in the steps to come. The layout of the roses and leaves is completely up to you, but varying the size of the flowers will help balance the overall pattern. I like to start with a large flower as the central part of the design and add smaller flowers around it.

(CONTINUED)

HOW TO SKETCH A ROSE

9. Start by sketching a teardrop shape with your cookie scribe—it can be as big or small as you like. This will form the rosebud.

10. To form the inner petals, add a small semicircle to the round end of the teardrop, slightly larger than the teardrop itself.

11. To each side of the teardrop, add a semicircle that begins at the point and ends near the semicircle on the round end of the teardrop. The more irregular the shapes, the more natural the rose petals will appear.

12. Add a semicircle under the last two you sketched, connecting the petals together. Feel free to add more outer petals to the rose and try experimenting by varying the shape and sizes of the semicircles so they do not all look identical.

HOW TO SKETCH A LEAF

13. Add leaves to the roses by sketching a curved arch that connects at the top and the bottom.

14. Add a stem to the inside that starts at the bottom and extends halfway up the center of the leaf. Each rose should have between two and three leaves.

HOW TO PIPE THE DESIGN

15. Using the Midnight Black Buttercream, pipe small dots along all the outlines you just sketched into the cake. These dots should resemble the shape of chocolate kisses (except tiny). Release pressure as you pull away to prevent the dots from forming "tails." Aim to keep them as short as possible. This process is very time consuming and will need to be done in stages as the cake warms to room temperature. Return the cake to the freezer for 15- to 20-minute intervals to rechill as needed. Also, be sure to place your piping bags in the fridge to cool along with it, as the heat from your hands will turn the buttercream warm and fluid.

16. Using the red buttercream, pipe small dots to fill in all the rose petals.

17. Using the turquoise buttercream, pipe small dots into all the leaves.

18. Finally, fill the space in between the flowers and leaves with the pink buttercream.

The cake is freshest if kept in the refrigerator until 1 hour before serving and is best if eaten within 3 days.

TIPS

*   Instead of using extra red coloring to achieve a deeper shade (this often makes the buttercream bitter and will stain your mouth), it is best to prepare the red buttercream a few hours ahead of time and allow the color to mature. The longer it sits the darker it will become.

*   Only a small amount of the Midnight Black Buttercream will be used for this design. Store any unused buttercream in an airtight container and use later to frost cupcakes or for other projects.

ANTOINETTE

MAKES 1 DOUBLE-TIERED CAKE

SERVES 30 TO 35

Let them eat cake! This design uses Lambeth-style piping, a classic style in the cake decorating world. The addition of glittery cherries gives it some modern flair, while still maintaining its elegance and sophistication. This style can be as extravagant as you choose; simply use smaller piping tips and add more detail. The layers are made up of Cherry Chip Cake with a hint of almond, filled with dark chocolate ganache, all frosted in Glossy Vanilla Buttercream.

2 batches Cherry Chip Cake batter (unbaked) (page 16)

2 batches Glossy Vanilla Buttercream (page 151)

Wilton delphinium blue gel coloring

1 batch Dark Chocolate Ganache Frosting (page 163)

Chefmaster pink gel coloring

Super Streusel gold balls

6 maraschino cherries, stems attached

Roxy & Rich pink edible glitter

TOOLS

3 (6" [15-cm]) round cake pans

3 (8" [20-cm]) round cake pans

4 or 5 piping bags

Wilton piping tips 2D, 6B and no. 10

1 (10" [25-cm]) cake board

1 (6" [15-cm]) cake board

Bubble tea straws

Bowl or cookie cutter, for tracing

PREP

1. Prepare the three 6-inch (15-cm) and three 8-inch (20-cm) round cake pans according to the directions on page 12. Prepare the Cherry Chip Cake batter. Divide the cake batter evenly among the prepared pans and bake according to the directions on page 15.

2. Prepare the Glossy Vanilla Buttercream. Divide the buttercream equally between two bowls and add ¼ teaspoon of delphinium blue gel coloring to one of the bowls; set aside. This will be used to frost the bottom tier.

3. Prepare the Dark Chocolate Ganache Frosting and, once completely set, transfer to a piping bag with the end snipped off. This will be used to fill the cakes.

4. From the second bowl of uncolored buttercream, transfer 1 cup (300 g) of buttercream to a piping bag fitted with the 2D tip, 1 cup (300 g) of buttercream to a piping bag fitted with the no. 10 tip and 1 cup (300 g) of buttercream to a piping bag fitted with the 6B tip. These will be used to pipe the details.

5. Color the remaining uncolored buttercream with 2 or 3 drops of pink gel coloring.

ASSEMBLY

6. With the Dark Chocolate Ganache Frosting, fill and stack the 6-inch (15-cm) cake onto the 6-inch (15-cm) cake board as well as the 8-inch (20-cm) cake onto the 10-inch (25-cm) cake board using the classic method as directed on page 30.

7. Using the pink buttercream, crumb coat the 6-inch (15-cm) cake and using the blue buttercream, crumb coat the 8-inch (20-cm) cake, according to the directions on page 34.

8. After chilling, add the final coat of pink to the 6-inch (15-cm) cake and a final coat of blue to the 8-inch (20-cm) cake, according to the directions on page 34.

9. Return the cakes to the turntable once they are well chilled. Insert three or four bubble tea straws or dowels into the 8-inch (20-cm) cake, and carefully place the 6-inch (15-cm) cake on top of it. See page 30 for full cake-stacking instructions.

(CONTINUED)

DECORATE

10. Using the 2D piping bag of uncolored buttercream, pipe a shell border along the base of each tier, as well as along the very top edge. To pipe a shell border to the top edge, hold the bag at an angle with the tip pointing away from you. The longest side of the tip should line up with the edge of the cake and be held slightly above the surface. Squeeze the bag as you flick your wrist upward and outward to form a closed C shape. Pipe these loops in a continuous border running lengthwise, each loop slightly overlapping the tail of the previous loop. End the border when you return to where you began piping. It will take some practice piping shells onto the side of the cake, so don't be afraid to practice on a separate cake or on parchment paper until you feel confident enough to pipe directly onto the cake.

11. Along the top edges of both tiers, trace semicircle outlines using a bowl or large cookie cutter. You will use this guide to pipe a garland-shaped border in the next step. Once the outlines have been made along both tiers, trace a smaller bowl or cookie cutter inside each of the larger semicircles.

12. Using the no. 10–tipped bag of uncolored buttercream, hold it at a 45-degree angle to the cake and pipe a line along the marked semicircles to create a double garland–style border. Repeat this along the top edges of both tiers.

13. Using the 6B-tipped bag of uncolored buttercream, pipe a single shell (closed C-shaped loop) upward in each place the garland border joins together. Be sure to release pressure as you pull away to create a clean point on each shell.

14. Using the no. 10–tipped bag of uncolored buttercream, pipe a small dot under each single shell on the bottom tier. On the top tier, pipe dots under each of the single shells, alternating between one dot and two dots running vertically.

15. Place a gold ball onto the point on each single shell.

16. Dip the cherries in the pink edible glitter and place on top of the cake, evenly spaced.

The cake is freshest if kept in the refrigerator until 1 hour before serving and is best if eaten within 3 days.

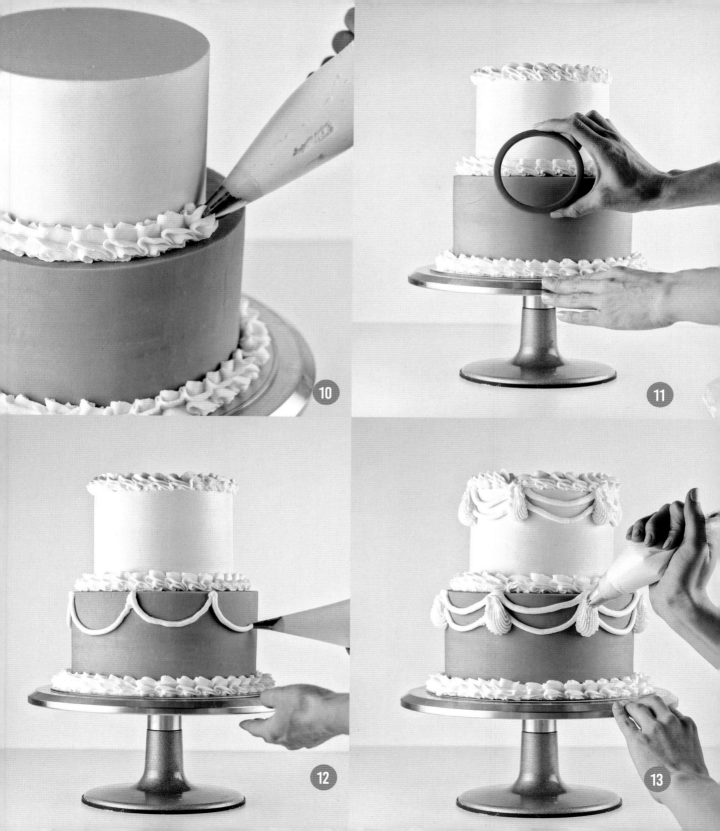

ON POINT

EYE-CATCHING GEODE CAKES

Geode cakes spiked in popularity in the early 2010s and still seem to be holding their place in the cake industry today! These days there are so many variations of this technique, and the design has spilled over to cupcakes, cookies, macarons and every other confection! Another cake trend worth noting is the #faultlinecake, which started a massive online whirlwind. Traditionally, geode cakes are adorned in beautifully colored rock candies to replicate actual crystals, but we will utilize some unexpected elements to switch things up. Get ready to create something unique with a guaranteed wow factor!

LADY PERSEPHONE

MAKES ONE 6-INCH (15-CM), 4-LAYER SQUARE CAKE

SERVES 30

From her glowing red crystals to her sleek black edges, this cake guarantees you will be coming back for more! Square cakes are so eye catching, as are geode cakes, which makes this such an iconic design. I replaced the regular rock candy with pomegranate arils, which resemble blood-red rubies. As you'd imagine, they are a lot easier to eat than hard rock candy and pair amazingly with Decadent Chocolate Cake and Pomegranate Buttercream. Frosting a square cake does take some patience, but the outcome is quite magnificent!

1 batch Decadent Chocolate Cake batter (unbaked) (page 139)

1 batch Pomegranate Buttercream (page 154; see Tip)

1 to 2 batches Midnight Black Buttercream (page 157)

2 fresh pomegranates

Piping gel

Edible gold leaf

Gold edible luster dust

Vodka or food-grade alcohol

TOOLS

4 (6" [15-cm]) square cake pans

2 (6¼" [16-cm]) square acrylic cake boards

Small, food-safe paintbrushes

Tweezers (optional)

PREP

1. Prepare four 6-inch (15-cm) square pans, using the same method as for round pans, according to the directions on page 12. Prepare the Decadent Chocolate Cake batter. Divide the batter equally among the prepared pans, and bake according to the directions on page 139.

2. Prepare the Pomegranate Buttercream and transfer 2 cups (600 g) to a piping bag with the end snipped off. This will be used to fill the cake. Prepare the Midnight Black Buttercream.

ASSEMBLY

3. Place the first layer, leveled side up, onto one of the square acrylic boards, and using the classic method outlined on page 30, fill with the Pomegranate Buttercream. Continue filling and stacking your layers, placing the last layer leveled side down.

4. Crumb coat your cake with the Midnight Black Buttercream, following the same directions for crumb coating a round cake as outlined on page 34.

5. Return the cake to the turntable once it is chilled. Place the second acrylic board on top of the cake, lining it up with the bottom board.

6. With your offset spatula, generously apply the Midnight Black Buttercream to the cake. Pay special attention to the corners, applying extra buttercream, as this area is the most compromised structurally.

7. Hold your bench scraper at a 45-degree angle to the cake and run it in a firm swipe across each panel, scraping against the edges of the boards. Be sure to clean off your scraper between swipes to avoid reapplying excess buttercream back onto the cake.

8. It is best to work in stages, as it is not likely you will be able to achieve a super-clean finish on the first coat. Place the cake back in the freezer for 10- to 15-minute intervals, just long enough to chill the surface. Once chilled, continue to reapply buttercream and scrape until the sides are smooth and the corners are sharp. Make sure the acrylic boards are perfectly lined up during this process to avoid a crooked cake. Chill in the freezer for approximately 20 minutes, or in the refrigerator for 3 to 4 hours.

9. Return the cake to the turntable, and using a sharp knife, run the blade under the acrylic board on the top of the cake to loosen. Carefully remove the board from the cake, trying your best to keep the sharp edge intact.

(CONTINUED)

10. Apply buttercream to the top of the cake, smoothing clean with your bench scraper. You may need to clean up the top edge with your offset spatula if there is any overhang. Don't worry if it looks like the cake is messy again after adding frosting on top. You can always place the cake in the freezer to chill slightly and reestablish those sharp corners once the buttercream has set up underneath.

DECORATE

11. Using a sharp knife, slice a large piece out of the top right corner of the cake. Cut the cake at a 45-degree angle so it is shallower in depth. I created a second cutout on one of the bottom corners, but you can start with one, if you'd like.

12. With your offset spatula, apply Midnight Black Buttercream to the exposed cake areas. Be careful not to spread any of the crumbs outside the cutouts. If you need to, feel free to rechill the cake to make the process cleaner and easier.

13. Remove the arils from one of the pomegranates, and place on a sheet of paper towel to absorb any excess juice. One by one, place the arils directly into the cutouts on the cake. They should stick to the buttercream, but if your buttercream is no longer sticky, apply a little bit of piping gel to help them stay in place.

14. Tear off small pieces of gold leaf by securing the sheet with a brush and pulling sections upward with a second brush or tweezers. Apply the small pieces of gold leaf along the edges of the holes, creating a border. Alternatively, this could be painted on with luster dust if you don't have gold leaf on hand.

15. In a small bowl, combine approximately ¼ teaspoon of luster dust and ½ to 1 teaspoon of vodka, mixing well. With your paintbrush, lightly splatter the gold mixture onto the cake using a flicking motion. For a finer mist of gold, run your thumb along the bristles of the paintbrush, allowing the paint to spray onto the cake. This works best with a firm-bristled brush or even a (brand-new) toothbrush.

16. Cut the second pomegranate in half and one of the halves in quarters, dabbing off any excess juice with a paper towel. Position one half and one quarter on top of the cake and, using some of the leftover gold mixture, brush lightly for a gilded effect.

The cake is freshest if kept in the refrigerator until 1 hour before serving and is best if eaten within 3 days.

TIP

* Store any leftover Pomegranate Buttercream in an airtight container in the refrigerator; the fresh fruit could cause it to spoil quickly.

ROSE QUARTZ GEODE

MAKES ONE 6-INCH (15-CM), 4-LAYER ROUND CAKE

SERVES 10 TO 12

Rose quartz is said to be the stone of love. This cake aims to capture the raw beauty this gem emanates, with the added advantage of being deliciously edible. Using a silicone mold to form the crystals makes this cake very simple to create, and with a dusting of edible glitter, it will take on an almost holographic effect. This cake boasts fluffy vanilla layers filled with Pistachio Buttercream and raspberry preserves for a surprisingly delightful indulgence.

1 batch Classic Vanilla Cake
(page 15)

1 batch Glossy Vanilla Buttercream
(page 151)

½ batch Pistachio Buttercream
(page 154)

¼ cup (60 g) high-quality raspberry preserves

1 to 2 (12- to 24-oz [340- to 680-g]) bags Wilton pink candy melts

Fancy Sprinkles pink and blue edible glitter

Edible gold leaf

TOOLS

Silicone crystal molds (see Tip)

Food-safe paintbrushes

Tweezers (optional)

PREP

1. Prepare the Classic Vanilla Cake, making four 6-inch (15-cm) cake layers, and the Glossy Vanilla Buttercream.

2. Prepare the Pistachio Buttercream. Transfer 2 cups (600 g) to a piping bag with the end snipped off. This will be used to fill the cake.

ASSEMBLY

3. Using the classic method outlined on page 30, fill and stack your cake with the Pistachio Buttercream, spreading 1 tablespoon (15 g) of the raspberry preserves between each layer on top of the buttercream for extra flavor.

4. Crumb coat and final coat your cake with the Glossy Vanilla Buttercream, according to the instructions on page 34.

HOW TO MAKE THE CRYSTALS

5. In a microwave-safe bowl, microwave the candy melts for 30-second intervals, stirring in between, until completely melted.

6. Once melted, pour the candy melts into the clean crystal molds. Shake and tap the molds to help the melts get into all the crevices and release any air bubbles. Place the filled molds on a tray and chill in the refrigerator to harden, about 10 minutes. Depending on how many molds you have, you may have to repeat this process several times until you have enough crystals to cover the cutout you will make in the cake. It took about 20 individual pieces in variously sized clusters to fill the area on my cake.

7. Once set, very carefully peel the pink crystals from the molds. There will be some delicate pieces, so it is best to use extra care when removing.

8. Lightly dust each crystal with the edible glitter to give them some shine. I dusted some using both pink and blue for a slightly purple hue. Tap to release any excess glitter and set aside.

(CONTINUED)

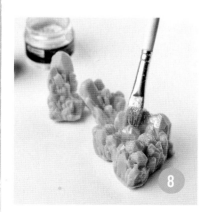

ROSE QUARTZ GEODE (CONTINUED)

HOW TO DECORATE THE CAKE

9. Return your cake to the turntable. Starting at the top and working down toward the base, cut out a large section of cake using a sharp knife. The cutout can be as big or as small as you like, but should resemble the basic shape of a pizza slice. Instead of slicing directly into the cake, cut it at a 45-degree angle so it is shallower in depth. If desired, cut out a second piece at the base.

10. With your offset spatula, apply Glossy Vanilla Buttercream to the exposed cake areas. Be careful not to spread any of the crumbs outside the hole. If you need to, feel free to rechill the cake to make the process cleaner and easier.

11. Starting in the center of the hole, press the pink crystals directly into the buttercream. Create a row of crystals that extend the length of the cutout. Begin working your way outward from the center, adding more crystals. This will seem more like a jigsaw puzzle at first. Try to find pieces that fit together tightly; you may need to turn and angle them in different ways until they fit well. Feel free to break them apart and use single shards to fill any small areas as well as areas around the edges.

12. Allow a few pieces to extend higher on top to act as a topper of sorts.

13. Tear off small pieces of gold leaf by securing the sheet with a brush and pulling sections upward with a second brush or tweezers. Apply the small pieces of gold leaf along the edges of the holes, creating a border. Alternatively, this could be painted on with luster dust if you don't have gold leaf on hand.

The cake is freshest if kept in the refrigerator until 1 hour before serving and is best if eaten within 3 days.

TIP

- Silicone crystal molds can be found on Amazon or Etsy.

COLOMBIAN EMERALD FAULT LINE

MAKES ONE 6-INCH (15-CM),
4-LAYER ROUND CAKE

SERVES 10 TO 12

Taking inspiration from rich emerald green tones, this bedazzled fault line cake is both contemporary and striking. Decadent Chocolate Cake layers filled and frosted with Chocolate-Hazelnut Italian Meringue Buttercream, studded with an assortment of metallic green dragees for a touch of finesse.

1 batch Decadent Chocolate Cake (page 139)

1 batch Chocolate-Hazelnut Buttercream (page 154)

Roxy & Rich Maple Leaf powdered coloring plus ½ tsp water to dilute

Metallic sprinkles in green, blue and gold

Gold edible luster dust

Vodka or food-grade alcohol

TOOLS

Food-safe paintbrush

PREP

1. Prepare the Decadent Chocolate Cake, making four 6-inch (15-cm) cake layers. Prepare the Chocolate-Hazelnut Buttercream and transfer 2 cups (600 g) to a piping bag with the end snipped off. This will be used to fill the cake.

2. Place 1 teaspoon of Maple Leaf powdered coloring in a small bowl. Add ½ teaspoon of water and mix until well incorporated and no lumps remain. Add the diluted green mixture to the remaining 4 cups (1.2 kg) of Chocolate-Hazelnut Buttercream. Transfer 2 cups (600 g) of colored buttercream to a piping bag with the end snipped off. This will be used for the final coat.

ASSEMBLY

3. Fill and stack your cake with the uncolored Chocolate-Hazelnut Buttercream using the classic method outlined on page 30.

4. Crumb coat your cake using the green Chocolate-Hazelnut Buttercream, according to the directions on page 34.

5. Return your cake to the turntable and with your offset spatula, spread the green-colored buttercream in a ring around the middle of the cake. This will help the sprinkles adhere to the cake.

DECORATE

6. In a small bowl, combine the green, blue and gold sprinkles. Place 1 to 2 tablespoons (10 to 20 g) of sprinkles in your hand at a time and press them into the ring of buttercream. You will need to do this a few times to cover the entire ring.

7. Starting at the base of the cake, pipe two or three rings of green-colored buttercream, working upward until you reach the edge of the sprinkles.

8. Next, starting from the top of the cake and working downward, pipe another two or three rings until you reach the edge of the sprinkles. The thickness of the buttercream should extend out farther than the sprinkles, so add a thicker layer of buttercream, if needed. This will help prevent sprinkles from getting into the buttercream you just piped.

9. With the tall bench scraper, smooth out the green-colored buttercream, being careful not to push the buttercream into the sprinkles. Once the cake is mostly smooth, place in the freezer for 10 to 15 minutes to allow the outer layer of buttercream to harden.

10. Now that you have a good base, you can touch up any messy areas. Add extra leaf-colored buttercream and smooth again until you have a clean final coat. Don't worry if the edges around the sprinkles look jagged; this is what we are aiming for!

11. In a small bowl, combine approximately ¼ teaspoon of luster dust and ½ to 1 teaspoon of vodka, mixing well. With a small, food-safe paintbrush, paint the jagged edges of buttercream around the sprinkles to form a gold border.

The cake is freshest if kept in the refrigerator until 1 hour before serving and is best if eaten within 3 days.

SAPPHIRE BLUE

MAKES ONE 6-INCH (15-CM),
4-LAYER ROUND CAKE

SERVES 10 TO 12

Have you noticed by now that sprinkles are incredibly versatile? One of my favorite ways to use sprinkles is in a geode cake. Yes, you heard that correctly—using sprinkles in place of crystals. Maybe unorthodox, but certainly a fun way to switch up the trend. Top off this delicious lemon-blueberry cake with some fresh flowers for an effortlessly glamorous look.

1 batch Blueberry Filling (page 167)

1 batch Fluffy Lemon Cake (page 144)

1 batch Simple Vanilla Buttercream (page 18)

Chefmaster coal black gel coloring

Assorted blue metallic sprinkles

Orchids or other white flowers

TOOLS

Floral tape

PREP

1. Prepare the Blueberry Filling. Once set, transfer to a piping bag with the end snipped off; this will be used to fill the cake. Prepare the Fluffy Lemon Cake, making four 6-inch (15-cm) cake layers.

2. Prepare the Simple Vanilla Buttercream and add 1 drop of coal black gel coloring. Transfer 1 cup (300 g) to a piping bag with the end snipped off. This will be used with the Blueberry Filling to fill the cake.

ASSEMBLY

3. Fill and stack your cake with the Blueberry Filling and Simple Vanilla Buttercream using the dam method as detailed on page 33.

4. Crumb coat and final coat your cake with the Simple Vanilla Buttercream, according to the directions on page 34. Allow the surface to remain somewhat rough to achieve a more authentic "concrete" look.

DECORATE

5. Return your cake to the turntable and, starting at the top of the cake, cut out a large section of cake using a sharp knife. The cutout can be as big or as small as you like, but it should resemble the basic shape of a pizza slice. Instead of slicing directly into the cake, cut it at a 45-degree angle so it is shallower in depth.

6. With your offset spatula, apply Simple Vanilla Buttercream to the exposed cake area. Be careful not to spread any of the crumbs outside the hole. If you need to, feel free to rechill the cake to make the process cleaner and easier.

7. Place 1 to 2 tablespoons (10 to 20 g) of sprinkles in your hand at a time, and carefully press them into the hole. You may have to place some sprinkles in any areas you missed by hand. Just be sure to cover as much of the hole with the sprinkles as possible.

8. Wrap the orchid stem in floral tape and press into the top. Allow the flowers to fall over the edge of the cake.

The cake is freshest if kept in the refrigerator until 1 hour before serving and is best if eaten within 3 days.

PAINT LIKE A PRO

ARTFUL EXPRESSIONS INSPIRED BY NATURE

In this chapter, unleash your inner Leonardo da Vinci by allowing the cake to become your canvas and buttercream your medium. You will learn to master the art of buttercream painting in its many forms. Using a palette knife to achieve beautiful watercolors, we will be covering all the basics. Oh, and don't worry if you skipped art class in high school; this does not require any former experience—just you, a paintbrush and an ample supply of creativity.

NIGHT FLOWERS

MAKES ONE 6-INCH (15-CM), 4-LAYER ROUND CAKE

SERVES 10 TO 12

With rich tones thoughtfully painted onto a black canvas, this cake is styled after the beautiful art of the Dutch Golden Age. In this tutorial, we use palette knives to create a beautifully textured masterpiece using buttercream to paint with. The first time I tried painting onto a cake, I was immediately in love. The process is so therapeutic and is more about capturing the essence of an image rather than realism. This type of art is so forgiving, you can't really do any wrong.

1 batch Decadent Chocolate Cake (page 139)

1 batch Midnight Black Buttercream (page 157)

1 batch Dark Chocolate Ganache Frosting (page 163)

½ batch Glossy Vanilla Buttercream (page 151)

Chefmaster burgundy, peach, avocado, forest green, gold, violet, pink and red gel coloring

Callebaut Dark Chocolate Crispearls

Red, blue, gold and green sprinkle beads

TOOLS

Metal palette knives in assorted sizes

PREP

1. Prepare the Decadent Chocolate Cake, making four 6-inch (15-cm) cake layers, and Midnight Black Buttercream. Prepare the Dark Chocolate Ganache Frosting and, once set, transfer to a piping bag with the end snipped off. This will be used to fill the cake.

2. Prepare the Glossy Vanilla Buttercream and divide it equally among 8 bowls, about 2 to 3 tablespoons (40 to 60 g) each. Add 5 drops of burgundy gel coloring to the first bowl, 1 drop of burgundy gel to the second, 2 drops of peach gel to the third, 3 drops of avocado gel to the fourth, 3 drops of forest green gel to the fifth, 2 drops of gold gel to the sixth, 6 drops of violet gel to the seventh and finally, 7 drops of pink, 3 drops of red and 1 drop of burgundy gel to the eighth bowl.

ASSEMBLY

3. Using the classic method as outlined on page 30, fill and stack your cake with the Dark Chocolate Ganache Frosting, sprinkling 1 tablespoon (10 g) of Crispearls between each layer for some extra flavor and a bit of crunch.

4. Crumb coat and final coat your cake with the Midnight Black Buttercream, according to the instructions on page 34.

DECORATE

5. Return the cake to the turntable, and using a small- to medium-sized palette knife, begin painting on the flowers in the different colors.

HOW TO PAINT A FLOWER

6. Dip the blade of a medium-sized palette knife in the colored buttercream. Not a lot is needed, and it should only cover the surface of the tip of the blade. To paint the first petal, hold your knife upright at a 45-degree angle and smear the buttercream onto the cake in a small semicircle. Pretend you are forming the shape of a moon and smear with the blade flat against the cake instead of digging in the tip. In a second movement with a flat blade, smear the semicircle of buttercream widthwise to form more of an oval.

7. Repeat this process to create another three or four additional petals to form a full flower. Each petal should slightly overlap the last one, and the ends of each petal should meet in the center. Feel free to trace an outline of the petals before painting, if that makes it a little easier to visualize.

(CONTINUED)

8. Dip the very tip of your blade in the gold-colored buttercream and lightly dab it on the center of the finished flower to add pollen. Feel free to skip this step and just leave the centers bare, if you prefer.

9. Place a sprinkle bead in the center of the flower.

10. Start painting flowers at the base of the right-hand side of the cake, working diagonally upward toward the top left-hand side. The flowers should continue slightly wrapping around the top of the cake in a crescent moon shape. Vary the size and colors of the flowers and try to balance the layout by painting 2 or 3 large flowers surrounded by lots of smaller flowers. Include a few single petals in between the flowers to fill in any empty spaces. Keep in mind you will be adding leaves, so allow enough room between the flowers for them.

HOW TO PAINT A LEAF

11. Add one to three leaves to each flower using a small- to medium-sized palette knife. Painting a leaf follows the same technique as painting a single petal, except you will use the green shades of buttercream. Feel free to make the leaves pointed, or wider and rounded to suit your preference. Refer to the Tips on how to achieve different shapes with your palette knife.

12. Place sprinkles in between the flowers to add a pop of color and some extra texture.

TIPS

- Don't forget to wipe your knife after each use, or at least to scrape off any excess.

- If you want the petals to be more pointed, either use a narrower knife or start higher up and make the widthwise smear less prominent. Once you've practiced this a few times, you'll be able to do it all in one swift movement.

- You can easily create different types of flowers by using different-sized and -shaped palette knives. For example, to create a flower with long petals (such as a daisy), you would use a thin, pointy palette knife and swipe it downward, instead of flaring it out.

- Give each individual petal lots of texture and try as much as possible to avoid blending the petals together. The amount of texture you use is ultimately dependent on your preference, and whether you prefer a raised, thick texture or more subtle texture. Use more buttercream on your knife while painting for thicker application.

- To add more dimension to your petals, you could add a secondary color close to the shade of the main color. I like to add a light smudge of white to pink flowers, pink to a purple flower, yellow to an orange flower and so on. Blend the secondary color into the first one by gently smearing with your knife. The more blended the colors, the more natural it will appear.

- Angle is everything! The angle at which your palette knife is held will greatly determine the shape of whatever you are painting. Practice smearing buttercream, holding the knife upside down, to the left, to the right and completely vertical.

- Using the edge of the blade will create a thin line, whereas using the entire flat area of the blade will result in a wider arrowhead-like shape.

- You will only need a small amount of buttercream to paint with, but place any leftovers into an airtight container to use for other projects later on! It's always helpful to have extra buttercream on hand.

LAKE OF SHINING WATERS

MAKES ONE 8-INCH (20-CM), 3-LAYER ROUND CAKE

SERVES 10 TO 12

If Bob Ross decorated cakes, this is what I picture them to look like. With tangy Lime Curd nestled between fluffy vanilla layers, this cake is coated and painted in a beautifully glossy buttercream to resemble a peaceful sunset over a lake of shimmering waters. This cake is much wider and shorter than the ones we have created thus far. The designs on this cake will be primarily focused on the top rather than the sides.

1 batch Lime Curd (page 172)

1 batch Classic Vanilla Cake (page 15)

1 batch Glossy Vanilla Buttercream (page 151)

Chefmaster violet, fuchsia, peach, sky blue and lemon yellow gel coloring

Wilton whitener gel

Water

TOOLS

3 (8" [20-cm]) round cake pans

Metal palette knives in assorted sizes

Stiff, food-safe paintbrush

PREP

1. Prepare the Lime Curd. Once set, transfer to a piping bag with the end snipped off. This will be used to fill the cake. Prepare the Classic Vanilla Cake using your three 8-inch (20-cm) prepared cake pans.

2. Prepare the Glossy Vanilla Buttercream. Divide ½ cup (150 g) of the buttercream equally among 5 small bowls. Add 2 drops of violet gel coloring to the first bowl, 2 drops of fuchsia gel to the second bowl, 1 drop of peach gel to the third bowl, 2 drops of sky blue gel to the fourth bowl and 2 drops of lemon yellow gel to the fifth bowl. Cover and set aside until ready to use.

ASSEMBLY

3. With the remaining uncolored Glossy Vanilla Buttercream and Lime Curd Filling, fill and stack your cake using the dam method as detailed on page 33.

4. Crumb coat and final coat your cake with the uncolored Glossy Vanilla Buttercream, according to the directions on page 34. Reserve 1 to 2 tablespoons (20 to 40 g) of the uncolored buttercream to use for painting later.

DECORATE

5. Return your cake to the turntable and with a ruler or bench scraper, mark a straight line across the middle of the cake. This will be used as a guide while painting.

6. Using a large palette knife and working from side to side, smear the violet buttercream onto the upper section of the cake, 2 to 3 inches (5 to 8 cm) down from the top. It does not need to be completely smooth; rather, leave some texture from your palette knife.

7. Smear a second section of fuchsia buttercream directly under the violet buttercream, extending down 1 to 2 inches (2.5 to 5 cm) farther. Blend where the colors meet to create a smooth transition. Be sure to clean your knife in between painting colors.

8. Smear a third section directly under the fuchsia using the peach buttercream and extend it to the central line. Try your best to keep the line straight. You can place a piece of parchment paper over the line to create a sharp horizon line. Blend where the colors meet to create a smooth transition.

(CONTINUED)

9. Lightly apply a small amount of yellow on top of the peach buttercream on only the left-hand side to indicate the sun's reflection. This area should only take up approximately ⅓ of the width of the peach section.

10. After adding the peach and yellow buttercream, fill in the bottom half of the cake with the blue buttercream.

11. With a clean palette knife, lightly apply a small amount of uncolored buttercream to the blue buttercream, to give the waves more dimension. Be sure to use uneven strokes and texture to make the waves look more natural and realistic.

12. Repeat this process on the violet section, applying uncolored buttercream lightly to the sky to resemble clouds.

13. In a small bowl, combine a few drops of Wilton whitener gel with a few drops of water, and stir until well combined. Dip your stiff paintbrush in the diluted white mixture, and lightly flick it onto the sky area of your cake by running your thumb across the bristles. This will add more dimension to the sky.

14. With a palette knife or paintbrush, paint a circle near the top left-hand edge using the yellow buttercream. Once you have created the outline, fill in the circle completely with yellow to form the sun.

15. With a small palette knife, lightly apply a small amount of peach buttercream on top of the waves, directly under the sun. The peach buttercream should start with a width of approximately 2 inches (5 cm) and taper as it reaches the bottom of the cake. (The basic shape is an upside-down triangle.)

16. Lightly apply a small amount of yellow buttercream on top of the peach to give it more dimension and to resemble the reflections of the sun on the water.

17. Add a small amount of uncolored buttercream to only the center area of the reflections (peach and yellow area).

18. Using the fuchsia buttercream, paint a few small clouds near the sun, slightly overlapping to look as though they have moved in front of it. Use a light dabbing motion to give the clouds a subtle texture.

19. Continue the colors from the top of the cake down the sides to cover the white buttercream, if desired. I added a little bit of violet to the blue on the sides to give it a two-toned look.

The cake is freshest if kept in the refrigerator until 1 hour before serving and is best if eaten within 3 days.

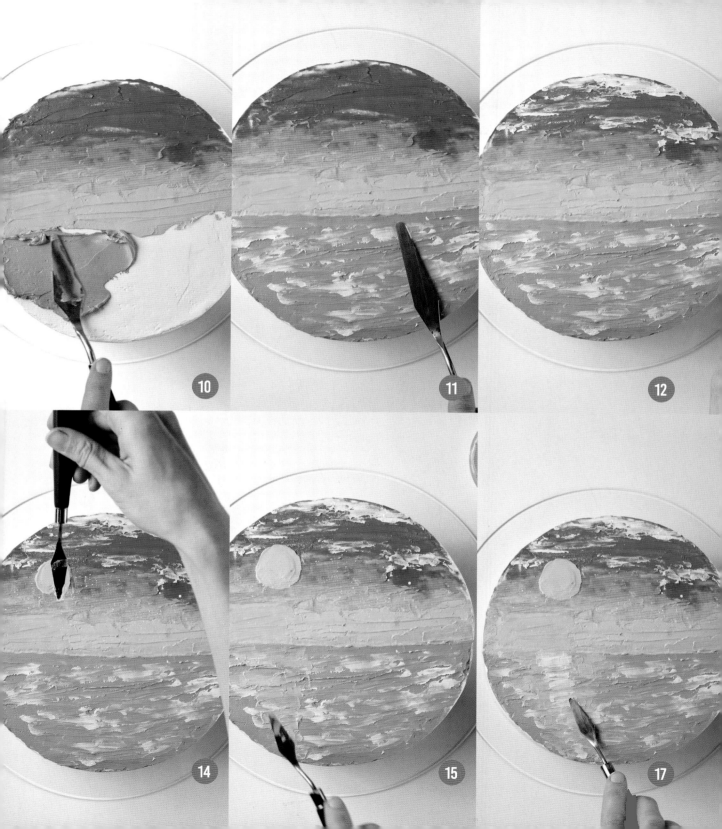

LA VIE EN ROSE

MAKES ONE 6-INCH (15-CM), 4-LAYER ROUND CAKE

SERVES 10 TO 12

There is nothing quite like gazing at the exquisitely beautiful stained-glass windows of a cathedral worn with time. Using buttercream, gel coloring and a bit of patience, you can achieve this breathtaking effect in cake form! Combine that with white chocolate ganache and raspberry cake layers, and it's destined to be a match made in heaven.

1 batch Raspberry Cake (page 16)

2 batches White Chocolate Ganache Frosting (page 160)

½ batch Midnight Black Buttercream (page 157; see Tips)

Raspberry preserves

Chefmaster sky blue, super red and/or pink and leaf green gel coloring

Vodka or food-grade alcohol

TOOLS

Wilton no. 3 piping tip

Food-safe paintbrushes (see Tips)

Paper towel or cotton swabs

PREP

1. Prepare the Raspberry Cake, making four 6-inch (15-cm) cake layers. Prepare the White Chocolate Ganache Frosting and, once set, transfer 1 cup (275 g) to a piping bag with the end snipped off. This will be used to fill and frost the cake.

2. Prepare the Midnight Black Buttercream and transfer 1 cup (300 g) to a piping bag fitted with the no. 3 tip. This will be used to pipe the outlines.

ASSEMBLY

3. Using the classic method outlined on page 30, fill and stack your cake with the White Chocolate Ganache Frosting, adding 1 tablespoon (15 g) of the raspberry preserves between each layer for extra flavor.

4. Crumb coat and final coat your cake with the White Chocolate Ganache Frosting, according to the directions on page 34.

HOW TO PIPE A FLOWER

5. Return the cake to the turntable. Start by piping a teardrop shape onto the front of the cake using the Midnight Black Buttercream. It can be as big or small as you like, as it will form the center of the rose.

6. To form the inner petals, pipe a small semicircle onto the round end of the teardrop, slightly larger than the teardrop itself.

7. To each side of the teardrop, add a semicircle that begins at the point and ends near the semicircle on the round end of the teardrop. The more irregular the shapes, the more natural the rose petals will appear.

8. Add a semicircle under the last two you piped, connecting the petals together. Feel free to add more outer petals to the rose and try experimenting by varying the shape and sizes of the semicircles, so they do not all look identical. Refer to the photos on page 85 on how to sketch a rose.

HOW TO PIPE A LEAF

9. Add leaves to the roses by piping a curved arch with the Midnight Black Buttercream, which connects at the top and the bottom. Each rose outline should have between two and three leaves. Refer to the photos on page 85 on how to sketch leaves.

(CONTINUED)

10. Continue to pipe these rose outlines all over the cake, varying the height and size of the petals. Feel free to pipe in some smaller buds as well as the larger roses. Allow some of the flowers and leaves to extend up to the top edge of the cake.

11. Using the Midnight Black Buttercream, pipe connecting lines in between the flowers and leaves. These pieces in between the flowers will look like the individual stained-glass shards. You can pipe as many or as few connecting lines as you would like, but keep in mind that you will need to paint the inside of each section, which can become quite time consuming! Leave some exposed space near the top of the cake, if desired. Place the cake in the fridge or freezer to firm up while you mix your paints.

HOW TO PAINT THE STAINED GLASS

12. Place 1 to 2 drops each of the blue, red/pink and green gel coloring in separate small bowls. To each bowl, add approximately 1 teaspoon of vodka. Mix each until each gel coloring has fully dissolved in the alcohol. There may be a few pieces that separate and float to the top—you can easily remove any pieces with a spoon or paintbrush.

13. With a paintbrush, paint inside the leaves using the green mixture. The more alcohol used in the mixture, the lighter the color will be. If you want the color to be dark and more solid rather than translucent, add extra gel coloring to your paint mixture. Be careful to avoid adding too much of the mixture to the stained-glass pieces, or droplets will form and run (see Tips). You can catch these drops before they spill onto the cake with a piece of paper towel or cotton swab.

14. Using the red/pink mixture, paint the inner sections of the roses.

15. Next, using the blue mixture, fill in all the individual stained-glass sections in between the flowers and leaves.

The cake is freshest if kept in the refrigerator until 1 hour before serving and is best if eaten within 3 days.

TIPS

- You will want to keep your cake well chilled while painting, as it will become more difficult to paint as the surface softens. Place in the freezer for 10- to 15-minute intervals during the decorating process to avoid this.

- Use a soft-bristled paintbrush to avoid damaging the surface of the cake while painting.

- Vary the shades of the three colors by further diluting the paints as you go. This will add a lot of dimension even though you are only using the three main colors. If the paint did not completely cover the surface the first time, you may have to go over it a second time to fill in any sparsely colored areas.

- Apply the paint using light pressure, with your brush flat against the surface instead of pointed, to avoid puncturing the surface with small holes.

- Use a different paintbrush to paint on the different colors or clean your brush well before switching.

- You will only need a small amount of Midnight Black Buttercream to pipe the outlines, but place any leftovers in an airtight container to use for other projects later on! It's always helpful to have extra buttercream on hand.

CALL OF THE SIREN

MAKES ONE 6-INCH (15-CM), 4-LAYER ROUND CAKE

SERVES 10 TO 12

Believe it or not, the design of this cake was based on a bottle of shampoo! It was covered in a gorgeous mermaid scale pattern in shades of purple and turquoise, with gleaming accents of gold. This particular cake has been compared to the rainbow fish from the popular children's book, but it is open to interpretation! Using an offset spatula to "paint" on the scales is a fairly straightforward technique that doesn't require much time or effort. The inside is especially delicious with a Cookies & Cream filling and fluffy vanilla cake layers.

1 batch Classic Vanilla Cake
(page 15; see Tip)

1 batch Simple Vanilla Buttercream
(page 18)

½ batch Cookies & Cream
Buttercream (page 20)

Chefmaster pink, teal and sky blue
gel coloring

Wilton Color Mist pink and blue
color sprays

Roxy & Rich edible pink and blue
glitter (optional)

Metallic blue sprinkles

Piping gel (optional)

Wilton white sugar pearls

Wilton silver edible cake paint

Zoi&Co seashell cake topper
(optional)

TOOLS

Large baking sheet

Paper towel

Fine-bristled, food-safe paintbrush

PREP

1. Prepare the Classic Vanilla Cake, making four 6-inch (15-cm) cake layers, and the Simple Vanilla Buttercream. Prepare the Cookies & Cream Buttercream and transfer it to a piping bag with the end snipped off. This will be used to fill and crumb coat the cake.

2. Divide the Simple Vanilla Buttercream equally among three bowls. Add 6 drops of Chefmaster pink gel coloring to the first bowl, 6 drops of teal gel to the second bowl and 6 drops of sky blue gel to the third bowl.

ASSEMBLY

3. Fill and stack your cake with the Cookies & Cream Buttercream using the classic method as outlined on page 30.

4. Crumb coat your cake with the Cookies & Cream Buttercream following the instructions on page 34.

HOW TO PAINT THE SCALES

5. Return your cake to the turntable and, with the pink-colored buttercream, spread a thin ring along the bottom edge using your offset spatula. This will prevent any white from showing through along the base.

6. Dip your offset spatula in the teal-colored buttercream, and with the blade of your spatula positioned at the base of the cake (tip pointed down), swipe the buttercream upward. The swipe should resemble the same shape as the blade of the spatula. Be sure to apply more pressure at the bottom of the swipe, and release pressure as you pull away at the top.

7. Repeat this process with the sky blue– and pink-colored buttercream, creating a sequence of different colors in a row along the base in whichever order you like. I didn't worry too much about making it into a perfect pattern, but you can do so if you prefer a more uniform look.

(CONTINUED)

8. Once you have finished the first row, begin on the second one directly above the last. This time, offset the colors and allow the "scales" to slightly overlap onto the previous row. If you started with pink the first time, begin with the teal or sky blue this time. Try to avoid stacking the same colors on top of each other. To achieve a purple hue on some scales, do not clean your spatula in between swipes. This will cause the colors to blend and create a more subtle transition between the shades.

9. Repeat steps 7 and 8, working your way up the cake in rows. When you get to the top edge of the cake, continue to add swipes toward the center until no white remains.

HOW TO BEDAZZLE

10. Place the cake on a large baking sheet lined with a paper towel. Shaking well before using, lightly spray a few sections of the cake with the blue color mist. This is just a light misting of color to select areas and is not intended to dramatically alter the color of the cake. In the areas left bare, lightly spray using the pink color mist. For more of a purple hue, allow the colors to slightly overlap. Refer to the color mist bottles for best spraying practices.

11. If desired, dust the blue-sprayed sections with blue glitter and repeat with the pink glitter on pink areas for a shimmery effect.

12. Press sprinkles onto 10 to 12 of the scales, covering each of them completely. If your buttercream has already crusted and the sprinkles are not sticking well, paint the scales with piping gel before applying the sprinkles. Fill in any holes or gaps between the scales with white sugar pearls. Place your cake in the freezer for 10 to 15 minutes to firm up before the next step.

13. Return your cake to the turntable and, using the silver edible paint and a fine-bristled paintbrush, outline each of the scales to help define their shape.

14. Add the seashell topper, if using.

The cake is freshest if kept in the refrigerator until 1 hour before serving and is best if eaten within 3 days.

TIP

•   For a fun flavor twist, add a few drops of green gel coloring and peppermint extract to the Classic Vanilla Cake batter before baking.

EXTRAVAGANT ELEMENTS

NEXT-LEVEL DESIGNS TO IMPRESS

Congratulations—you've made it, and all your hard work has certainly paid off! It is time to use everything you've learned thus far to create something incredible! The cakes laid out in this chapter focus on exciting new elements that you will learn to make from scratch. From chocolate spheres to decorated sugar cookies, I'm sure you'll find something to spark your creativity and get you excited to hit the kitchen! Just remember to take your time and have fun with it.

ENCHANTED FOREST

MAKES ONE 6-INCH (15-CM),
4-LAYER ROUND CAKE

SERVES 10 TO 12

Discover the secrets of an enchanted forest with this whimsical woodland design. An indulgent Black Forest cake covered in brushed chocolate and mossy accents, it is sure to capture you under its spell! There are many ways to create a tree stump effect, but in this tutorial, you will learn how to achieve it simply by using chocolate. Flora and berries are used to add to its ethereal charm, but feel free to incorporate more color for a touch of whimsy.

1 batch Cherry Filling (page 168)

1 batch Decadent Chocolate Cake (page 139)

1 batch Fudgy Chocolate Buttercream (page 148)

½ batch Simple Vanilla Buttercream (page 18; see Tip)

Chefmaster coal black gel coloring

1½ (10- to 15-oz [283- to 424-g]) bags Ghirardelli dark chocolate melting wafers

Fresh greenery, wax flowers and decorative berries

TOOLS

Wilton no. 125 piping tip

Parchment paper

Large, food-safe paintbrush

Floral tape (optional)

PREP

1. Prepare the Cherry Filling. Once set, transfer to a piping bag with the end snipped off. This will be used with the Fudgy Chocolate Buttercream to fill the cake.

2. Prepare the Decadent Chocolate Cake, making four 6-inch (15-cm) cake layers. Prepare the Fudgy Chocolate Buttercream, transferring 1 cup (300 g) to a piping bag with the end snipped off.

3. Prepare the Simple Vanilla Buttercream. In a small bowl, combine 1 cup (300 g) of Simple Vanilla Buttercream with 1 drop of coal black gel coloring. Transfer to a piping bag fitted with the no. 125 tip. This will be used to pipe on the bark mushrooms.

ASSEMBLY

4. Fill and stack your cake with the Fudgy Chocolate Buttercream and Cherry Filling using the dam method as directed on page 33.

5. Crumb coat and final coat your cake with the Fudgy Chocolate Buttercream, according to the directions on page 34.

6. Return the cake to the turntable. Run your spatula on top of the cake, starting along the top edge and working toward the center to create a swirl. The swirl should look like the rings in a tree stump. Chill in the freezer for approximately 20 minutes, or in the refrigerator for 3 to 4 hours.

MAKE THE CHOCOLATE BARK

7. While your cake is chilling, in a microwave-safe bowl, microwave the melting wafers for 20-second intervals until completely melted. Be sure to stir in between intervals to prevent the chocolate from burning on the bottom.

8. Lay down a piece of parchment paper and pour the melted chocolate onto it. Spread out the chocolate to about 1/16 inch (3 mm) thick using an offset spatula. Place a second piece of parchment paper directly on top of the melted chocolate.

9. Starting on the narrow end, roll up the parchment paper like a scroll. Set it aside to harden completely.

(CONTINUED)

DECORATE

10. Return the cake to the turntable. Gently unwrap the chocolate roll and separate some of the larger pieces.

11. Place the pieces of chocolate vertically on the cake, securing with a dot of the leftover buttercream if the shards have trouble sticking. Try to cover up as much of the buttercream with the chocolate as you can. You may need to break up the pieces to fit into smaller spots.

12. Place any leftover chocolate back in the microwave-safe bowl and re-melt. Using the large paintbrush, generously brush the melted chocolate onto all the shards covering the cake. You do not have to make it look perfectly smooth; it should be rough for a more natural appearance.

13. With the black gel–tinted buttercream, pipe a cluster of bark mushrooms onto the cake. Position the flat side of your piping tip horizontally with the opening touching the cake. Apply pressure, pulling the tip outward, creating a small buttercream "shelf." Release pressure as you pull away. Pipe an additional two or three buttercream shelves, making each one a little smaller than the one above it.

14. Cut small pieces of greenery and, if desired, wrap the ends in floral tape. Arrange the fresh greenery, wax flowers and decorative berries all around the cake.

The cake is freshest if kept in the refrigerator until 1 hour before serving and is best if eaten within 3 days.

TIP

• You will only need a small amount of buttercream to pipe the mushrooms, but place any leftovers into an airtight container to use for other projects later on! It's always helpful to have extra buttercream on hand.

COSMIC BUBBLES

MAKES ONE 6-INCH (15-CM), 4-LAYER ROUND CAKE

SERVES 10 TO 12

We all have that one friend who shows up to the party overdressed, but somehow pulls it off with ease. This cake is that friend. With a certain pastel punk energy, this cake will divert everyone's attention straight toward the dessert table and won't disappoint in flavor with its tangy strawberry-infused filling.

1 batch Decadent Chocolate Cake (page 139)

1 batch Midnight Black Buttercream (using Method 2 recipe on page 159)

½ batch Strawberry Buttercream (page 154)

1 to 2 (10- to 20-oz [282- to 566-g]) bags Ghirardelli white chocolate melting wafers

Roxy & Rich pink and blue edible glitter

TOOLS

1 (2½" [6.25-cm]) sphere cavity mold

1 (1" [2.5-cm]) sphere cavity mold

Large, food-safe paintbrush

Ziplock bag

Magic Freeze Spray (recommended; see Tip)

PREP

1. Prepare the Decadent Chocolate Cake, making four 6-inch (15-cm) cake layers, and the Midnight Black Buttercream.

2. Prepare the Strawberry Buttercream and transfer 1 cup (300 g) to a piping bag with the end snipped off. This will be used to fill the cake.

ASSEMBLY

3. Fill and stack your cake with the Strawberry Buttercream using the classic method as detailed on page 30.

4. Crumb coat and final coat your cake with the Midnight Black Buttercream according to the directions on page 34.

5. While the cake is chilling, prepare the white chocolate spheres: Prep the molds by wiping each cavity with a microfiber cloth to get rid of any dust or crumbs.

MAKE THE CHOCOLATE SPHERES

6. In a microwave-safe bowl, microwave the melting wafers at 20-second intervals until completely melted. Be sure to stir in between intervals to prevent the chocolate from burning.

7. Working with one mold at a time, pour approximately 2 tablespoons (30 ml) of the melted chocolate into each cavity. Using upward strokes, coat the cavity evenly with a food-safe paintbrush.

8. Don't worry if some of the chocolate spills over the brim; this will be melted down later. If excess chocolate wells up in the cavity, turn the mold upside down on top of a piece of parchment paper. Allow the excess chocolate to run out of the mold onto the parchment. The chocolate needs to be thick enough to hold its shape without breaking, but still thin and light enough to stack during decorating. Feel free to add a very thin second layer if there are areas with uneven coverage.

9. Once fully coated, place the mold in the fridge to set for 10 minutes. Once chilled, gently remove the sphere halves from the molds by peeling away the silicone from the chocolate.

(CONTINUED)

10. It's now time to create the spheres. Heat a microwave-safe plate either in the microwave, or by placing an oven-safe plate in a preheated 200°F (93°C) oven for 2 to 5 minutes. Carefully touch the chocolate halves to the hot plate one at a time, open side down. Only melt until the half spheres have formed a clean edge. If melted too long, they will lose their spherical shape.

11. While the chocolate is still wet, gently press the two halves together to form a sphere, wiping away any excess chocolate along the seam. Allow the spheres to set fully before decorating.

12. Create three or four large spheres in total, leaving one or two of them in half. Create four to six small spheres in total, leaving one or two of them in half.

13. Place a chocolate sphere in a ziplock bag and add 1 teaspoon of glitter. Seal the bag and very gently shake to coat the sphere with glitter. Repeat this step with all the spheres, using both the pink and blue glitter. Tap each chocolate sphere to get rid of any excess glitter.

14. Reheat some of the leftover chocolate you used for the spheres, and place it in a piping bag with the very end snipped off. This will be used to attach the spheres to the cake.

DECORATE

15. Return the cake to the turntable. Pipe a dot of chocolate onto the very top of the cake and start by attaching a large sphere to the buttercream followed by one to two of the smaller spheres. It may take a few minutes to allow the chocolate to harden before adding more spheres, but you can spray with freeze spray to speed up the process. Continue attaching the smaller spheres to the larger spheres in the same manner, by piping a dot of chocolate and spraying to freeze them together.

16. Starting at the base of the cake, press a variety of large and small spheres directly into the buttercream, spraying to help them adhere, creating a diagonal line reaching to the top edge. Be sure to use a mix of half spheres and whole spheres.

The cake is freshest if kept in the refrigerator until 1 hour before serving and is best if eaten within 3 days.

TIP

• This process is a lot easier if you use Magic Freeze Spray to instantly chill the piped chocolate, connecting the spheres together. Magic Freeze Spray can be found on Amazon.

DRIPPING POISON APPLE

MAKES ONE 6-INCH (15-CM), 4-LAYER ROUND CAKE

SERVES 10 TO 12

Moist vanilla layers with spiced apple filling, velvet white as snow, topped with a crisp red apple dripping in chocolate—are you ready to take a bite? Learn how to achieve a unique velvet textured cake in this tutorial as well as a simple way to dip apples, which are easy to eat and taste divine.

1 batch Apple Filling (page 171)

1 batch Classic Vanilla Cake (page 15)

1 batch Glossy Vanilla Buttercream (page 151)

1 batch White Chocolate Ganache Drip (page 24)

Chefmaster super red gel coloring

White Velvet Spray (see Tip)

1 medium-sized red apple, washed well

TOOLS

Parchment paper

Natural twig or wooden skewer

PREP

1. Prepare the Apple Filling. Once set, transfer to a piping bag with the end snipped off. This will be used to fill the cake. Prepare the Classic Vanilla Cake, making four 6-inch (15-cm) cake layers.

2. Prepare the Glossy Vanilla Buttercream. Transfer 1 cup (300 g) of buttercream to a piping bag with the end snipped off. This will be used with the Apple Filling to fill the cake.

3. Prepare the White Chocolate Ganache Drip, adding ½ to 1 teaspoon of red gel coloring while the ganache is still warm.

ASSEMBLY

4. Fill and stack your cake with the Glossy Vanilla Buttercream and Apple Filling using the dam method as detailed on page 33.

5. Crumb coat and final coat your cake using the remaining Glossy Vanilla Buttercream, according to the directions on page 34.

DECORATE

6. Return the chilled cake to the turntable with a sheet of parchment paper beneath it. Starting at the base of the cake and working your way up, evenly spray the entire surface with the White Velvet Spray. Refer to the specific instructions on the can for best spraying practices.

7. Before using, refer to the instructions on page 25 to test whether the ganache has reached the correct consistency. Remove the stem from the apple and insert the twig or skewer into the top of the apple where the stem was previously.

8. Holding the apple by the twig, dip it in the ganache until coated. Hold the apple over the bowl until all the excess ganache has dripped off.

9. Place the coated apple onto the top of the cake, gently pressing it into the buttercream to secure.

10. With the leftover ganache, drizzle spoonfuls around the base of the apple, allowing some of the ganache to drip and run down the side of the cake.

The cake is freshest if kept in the refrigerator until 1 hour before serving and is best if eaten within 3 days.

TIP

- White Velvet Spray can be found in cake decorating supply stores or on Amazon.

24 KARAT

MAKES ONE 6-INCH (15-CM),
2-LAYER BUNDT CAKE

SERVES 10 TO 12

The idea for this cake came to me in the middle of the night, as many do! I pictured a glistening golden pumpkin sitting atop a tall pedestal, filled with spicy pumpkin layers with a rich caramel center. It worked out perfectly and may just be the most delicious out of all the recipes in this book—in my opinion, that is!

1 batch Dulce de Leche (page 176)

Vegetable shortening, for pans

All-purpose flour, for dusting

1 batch Pumpkin Spice Cake batter (unbaked) (page 147)

2 batches Dark Chocolate Ganache Frosting (page 163)

Gold edible luster dust

Vodka or food-grade alcohol

TOOLS

2 (8″ [20-cm]) Bundt pans

1 (10″ [25-cm]) cake board

Food-safe gloves

Plastic wrap

Large, food-safe paintbrush

PREP

1. Prepare the Dulce de Leche. Once set, transfer to a piping bag with the end snipped off. This will be used to fill the cake.

2. Grease the Bundt pans with vegetable shortening and dust with flour until well coated. Prepare the Pumpkin Spice Cake batter and divide it evenly between the prepared pans. Bake according to the directions on page 147.

3. Prepare the Dark Chocolate Ganache Frosting. Once set, transfer to a piping bag with the end snipped off. This will be used to frost the cake.

ASSEMBLY

4. Level the flat top of each cake with a large, serrated knife.

5. Spread 1 teaspoon of Dark Chocolate Ganache Frosting onto the cake board to help secure the cake on top. Place one of the cooled Bundt cakes on the cake board, leveled side up.

6. Pipe an even layer of Dulce de Leche onto the top of the cake, smoothing with an offset spatula. Place the second Bundt half on top of the first, leveled side down, sandwiching the two together. Fill the center cavity with the remaining Dulce de Leche.

DECORATE

7. Starting at the base of the cake, pipe on the ganache to form a final coat. Smooth it out using an offset spatula.

8. Swipe lines from the bottom of the pumpkin all the way to the top using your offset spatula. Make seven or eight swipes in total to form the segments of a pumpkin. I left the edges sharp for more of a geometric look, but feel free to smooth out the edges for a natural, more rounded appearance. For a rounded pumpkin, don a pair of gloves and smooth out the sharp edges with your fingers. Run from the bottom all the way up to the top. Place the frosted cake in the freezer to chill for approximately 20 minutes, or in the refrigerator 3 to 4 hours.

9. Pipe the remaining ganache onto a piece of plastic wrap and roll into a log shape; it should be relatively thick at this point. Place in the refrigerator to chill until firm. This will be used to create the pumpkin stem.

10. Once the ganache has set, unwrap and carve into a stemlike shape using a sharp knife. Slice lengthwise and widthwise in straight lines until about 2 inches (5 cm) in length, and 1 inch (2.5 cm) in width. Cut the top edge diagonally for a geometric look. Return the stem to the refrigerator until ready to place on the cake.

11. Return the cake to the turntable for painting. In a small bowl, combine 1 to 2 teaspoons (5 to 10 ml) of gold luster dust and 1 to 2 teaspoons (5 to 10 ml) of vodka. Stir with the paintbrush to get rid of any clumps. Starting at the base of the cake, paint the entire surface in the gold paint in upward strokes. It may take several coats to completely cover the chocolate ganache. If applying a second coat, allow the initial layer to dry completely before adding the final coat.

12. Place the chocolate stem in the center of the pumpkin as the finishing touch.

The cake is freshest if kept in the refrigerator until 1 hour before serving and is best if eaten within 3 days.

HOME FOR THE HOLIDAYS

MAKES 1 DOUBLE-TIERED CAKE

SERVES 18 TO 20

You need to create something a little extra at least once a year, and the holidays are always a good excuse! This multitiered sugar cookie village is set upon Cranberry Orange Cake layers, frosted with Glossy Vanilla Buttercream and sprinkled with glittery sanding sugar. This cake was highly inspired by the Sugar Plum Fairy and incorporates soft pastels, swirly sweets and fluffy snow.

1 batch Sugar Cookies dough
(unbaked) (page 180)

All-purpose flour, for dusting

1 batch Royal Icing (page 183;
see Tips)

Chefmaster pink, mint and sky blue
gel coloring

Bakery Bling Drenched in Diamonds
glittery sugar

Sprinkle Pop "Merry and Bright"
sprinkles

2 batches Cranberry Orange Cake
batter (unbaked) (page 16)

2 batches Glossy Vanilla
Buttercream (page 151)

Swirly lollipops, candy canes and
peppermints

TOOLS

Sugar Cookie Village template (printed from my website; more info on page 185)

Parchment paper

Scissors

Snowflake cookie cutters

Christmas tree cookie cutters

Large baking sheet

4 or 5 piping bags

Cookie scribe or toothpick

4 (4" [10-cm]) round cake pans

4 (6" [15-cm]) round cake pans

1 (4" [10-cm]) cake board

1 (8" [20-cm]) cake board

3 or 4 bubble tea straws or wooden dowels

MAKE THE COOKIES

1. Prepare the Sugar Cookie dough. Trace the sugar cookie village stencils onto parchment paper and cut out with scissors. Remove the chilled dough from the refrigerator and place on a floured surface. Roll out to approximately ¼ inch (6 mm) in thickness. Place the stencil cutouts on the dough, and with a sharp knife, cut out 12 house-shaped cookies. Using cookie cutters, create snowflakes and Christmas trees with the remaining dough. Place the cutout cookies onto an ungreased, large baking sheet and bake according to the directions on page 180.

2. Prepare the Royal Icing. Separate ¼ cup (35 g) of stiff-consistency royal icing into a piping bag and set aside. See page 183 for directions on creating different icing consistencies. This will be used to pipe the borders onto the cookies.

3. We will be using the remaining icing at a flooding consistency, which is thinner and is used to fill cookies. See page 183 for directions on creating different icing consistencies. Divide the thinned icing equally among three bowls. Add 1 drop of pink gel coloring to the first bowl, 1 drop of mint gel to the second bowl and 1 drop of sky blue gel to the third bowl. Transfer the colored icing to individual piping bags and snip a very small hole in the end of each.

4. Using your desired color of royal icing at flooding consistency, pipe an outline around the outer edge of each cookie. This will serve as a type of dam for the rest of the icing.

(CONTINUED)

5. Pipe into the center of each cookie using the same color to fill it in completely, in a back-and-forth motion. Pop any air bubbles using a cookie scribe and spread the icing until it has formed an even coat.

6. Pick up each cookie and gently shake it from side to side to allow the icing to settle into place. Sprinkle the cookies with glittery sugar and/or sprinkles while still wet for a frosty appearance. Allow the frosted cookies to dry for 2 to 3 hours, or until very dry to the touch. Once the cookies are completely dry, snip a very small hole into the end of the piping bag of the stiff-consistency icing. Pipe a white outline along the outer edge of the house panels.

MAKE THE CAKE

7. Prepare the 4-inch (10-cm) and 6-inch (15-cm) pans according to the directions on page 12. Prepare the Cranberry Orange Cake batter. Divide the cake batter evenly among the prepared pans. Bake the 4-inch (10-cm) rounds for 25 to 30 minutes and the 6-inch (15-cm) rounds for 30 to 35 minutes, according to the directions on page 15.

8. Prepare the Glossy Vanilla Buttercream. Transfer 1 cup (300 g) of buttercream into a piping bag with the end snipped off. This will be used to attach the cookies.

9. Fill and stack the 6-inch (15-cm) rounds onto the larger cake board with the Glossy Vanilla Buttercream using the classic method as outlined on page 30. Repeat the same filling and stacking process with the 4-inch (10-cm) cake layers.

10. Crumb coat and final coat both cakes with the Glossy Vanilla Buttercream, according to the directions on page 34.

DECORATE

11. Once the cakes are well chilled, return them to the turntable. Insert bubble tea straws into a 6-inch (15-cm) cake and stack a 4-inch (10-cm) cake directly on top. See page 36 for full stacking instructions.

12. Pipe buttercream onto the back of each cookie to act as glue, and press along the top and bottom tiers, allowing some of the pieces to overlap slightly.

13. Pipe "snow" ruffles of buttercream onto the top edge of each cookie.

14. Lightly apply the glittery sugar and sprinkles to the top tier, allowing some to fall onto the bottom tier to resemble falling snowflakes. Arrange the pieces of candy on both tiers.

The cake is freshest if kept in the refrigerator until 1 hour before serving and is best if eaten within 3 days.

TIPS

• The royal icing should slowly fall out of the piping bag when using. You should be able to pipe a line of icing without applying much pressure, using a pulling or dragging motion along the edges. If the line breaks while piping, this may be an indication that the icing is too thick. Add a few drops of water and test again for the correct consistency.

• Transfer unused icing to an airtight container and store in the refrigerator for 3 days, or in a ziplock bag in the freezer for up to 2 months.

5

6

12A

12B

14

RECIPES FOR SUCCESS

In this chapter, you will find a collection of my tried-and-true original recipes, including the highly sought-after Midnight Black Buttercream (page 157). These recipes can be used as the base for almost any flavor combination, which makes them the perfect starting point for anyone beginning their baking journey. I encourage you to create your own rendition of these recipes and consider this a foundation to build upon.

The first recipes you should aim to perfect are Classic Vanilla Cake (page 15) and Simple Vanilla Buttercream (page 18). Feel free to flip back to the Master the Basics chapter (page 9) for tips and tricks on preparation, flavor variations and best practices when baking.

DECADENT CHOCOLATE CAKE

MAKES FOUR 6-INCH (15-CM) OR THREE 8-INCH (20-CM) ROUND CAKE LAYERS

Chocolate cake is a classic in every family, and this recipe brings you right back home. With a fluffy texture and a healthy dose of chocolate, this cake will satisfy everyone's sweet tooth!

Vegetable oil spray, for pans

¾ cup (83 g) unsweetened cocoa powder plus 2 to 3 tbsp (11 to 16 g) for dusting

2½ cups (312 g) all-purpose flour

2½ cups (500 g) sugar

2 tsp (9 g) slightly heaped baking soda

1 tsp baking powder

1 tsp salt

3 large eggs, at room temperature

1 cup (240 ml) sour cream, at room temperature

½ cup (120 ml) vegetable oil

1 tbsp (15 ml) vanilla paste or pure vanilla extract

1 cup (240 ml) hot water

½ cup (85 g) high-quality dark chocolate chips

1. Preheat the oven to 350°F (176°C). Grease with vegetable oil spray, dust with cocoa powder and line four 6-inch (15-cm) or three 8-inch (20-cm) round cake pans with parchment paper, according to the directions on page 12.

2. Sift the flour, sugar, cocoa powder, baking soda, baking powder and salt into the bowl of your stand mixer fitted with the paddle attachment. Set the mixer on low speed, mixing until fully combined.

3. In a medium-sized bowl, combine the eggs, sour cream, oil and vanilla. Whisk until well incorporated, then set aside.

4. In a small saucepan, heat the water until just below the boiling point. While the water is heating, place the chocolate chips in a microwave-safe bowl and microwave for 30-second intervals, stirring in between, until melted completely.

5. With the mixer running on low speed, pour the egg mixture into the flour mixture in a slow and steady stream. Slowly add the hot water and melted chocolate. Increase your mixer speed to medium and beat until creamy, no longer than 1 to 2 minutes.

6. Divide the cake batter equally among the prepared pans. Bake for 30 to 35 minutes, or until a toothpick inserted into the center of a cake comes out clean and the cake has pulled away from the edges slightly. Remove from the oven and allow the cakes to cool in their pans for approximately 15 minutes before inverting onto wire racks or a clean countertop. Allow the layers to cool completely before filling and decorating.

TIPS

- Before starting, be sure all your ingredients are at room temperature. This will ensure that all the ingredients will blend and emulsify correctly, which will result in a light and fluffy cake.

- This recipe can easily be used for baking cupcakes. Pour the prepared batter into a cupcake tray (or trays) and bake for 18 to 21 minutes. Makes about 48 cupcakes.

ORANGE DREAM-SICLE CAKE

MAKES FOUR 6-INCH (15-CM) OR THREE 8-INCH (20-CM) ROUND CAKE LAYERS

This cake is the perfect treat on a hot summer day and would be incredible with a big scoop of vanilla ice cream on top! Forget boxed mix and orange gelatin—this cake recipe is made entirely from scratch and uses actual orange juice! It packs a ton of flavor and is incredibly moist and fluffy.

Vegetable oil spray, for pans

3 cups (375 g) all-purpose flour, plus more for dusting

1 cup (226 g) unsalted butter, at room temperature

2½ cups (500 g) sugar

4½ tsp (20 g) baking powder

¾ tsp sea salt

3 tbsp (18 g) King Arthur cake enhancer (optional)

1½ cups (360 ml) full-fat milk, at room temperature

7 large egg whites, at room temperature

1 tbsp (15 ml) pure vanilla extract

1 tsp orange extract

3 tbsp (45 ml) orange juice concentrate

Chefmaster sunset orange gel coloring

1. Preheat the oven to 350°F (176°C). Grease with vegetable oil spray, dust with flour and line four 6-inch (15-cm) or three 8-inch (20-cm) round cake pans with parchment paper, according to the directions on page 12.

2. In the bowl of your stand mixer fitted with the whisk attachment, beat the butter on high speed for 3 minutes, until fluffy. Lower the mixer speed to low and slowly pour in the sugar. Return the mixer to high speed and beat for an additional 5 minutes, or until pale, fluffy and increased in volume.

3. While the mixer is running, prepare the rest of your ingredients: Sift the flour, baking powder, salt and cake enhancer, if using, into a bowl and set aside.

4. In a separate bowl, whisk together the milk, egg whites, extracts and orange juice concentrate.

5. Set your mixer to the lowest setting, and alternating between the wet and dry ingredients, add 1 cup (130 g) of the flour mixture and 1 cup (240 ml) of the milk mixture to the stand mixer at a time. Increase the mixer to medium and beat until smooth, no longer than 1 to 2 minutes.

6. Transfer half of the batter to a separate bowl, and add a few drops of sunset orange gel coloring to that half. Gently mix until incorporated.

7. Scoop spoonfuls of batter into the prepared pans, alternating between the white and orange mixtures. Fill each pan half full. With a toothpick, swirl the colors together by running it through the batter.

8. Bake for 30 to 35 minutes, or until a toothpick inserted into the center of a cake comes out clean. Remove from the oven and allow the cakes to cool in their pans for approximately 10 minutes before inverting onto wire racks or a clean countertop. Allow the cake layers to cool completely before filling and decorating. Wrap the cake layers in plastic wrap and place in the fridge or freezer until ready to use.

TIPS

- Before starting, be sure all your ingredients are at room temperature. This will ensure that all the ingredients will blend and emulsify correctly and will result in a light and fluffy cake.

- This recipe can easily be used for baking cupcakes. Pour the prepared batter into a cupcake tray (or trays) and bake for 18 to 21 minutes, or until a toothpick inserted in the center of one comes out clean. Makes about 48 cupcakes.

RED VELVET
CAKE

MAKES FOUR 6-INCH (15-CM) OR THREE 8-INCH (20-CM) ROUND CAKE LAYERS

No one can really decide which flavor red velvet cake is, but everyone agrees it should be moist and spongy, tangy with a hint of cocoa and of course deep red in color. This recipe ticks all the boxes and delivers buttery soft layers, which pair deliciously with my Cream Cheese Frosting (page 164).

Vegetable oil spray, for pans

3 cups (375 g) all-purpose flour, plus more for dusting

3 cups (600 g) sugar

3 tbsp (22 g) unsweetened cocoa powder

2 tsp (9 g) baking soda

1 tsp salt

3 tbsp (18 g) King Arthur cake enhancer (optional)

½ cup (113 g) unsalted butter, melted

½ cup (120 ml) vegetable oil

3 large eggs, at room temperature

1½ cups (360 ml) buttermilk, at room temperature

3 tbsp (45 ml) sour cream, at room temperature

1 tbsp (15 ml) vanilla paste or pure vanilla extract

1 tbsp (15 ml) cider vinegar

1 tbsp (15 ml) Chefmaster super red gel coloring

1. Preheat the oven to 350°F (176°C). Grease with vegetable oil spray, dust with flour and line four 6-inch (15-cm) or three 8-inch (20-cm) round cake pans with parchment paper, according to the directions on page 12.

2. Sift the flour, sugar, cocoa, baking soda, salt and cake enhancer, if using, into the bowl of your stand mixer fitted with the paddle attachment. Set the mixer to the lowest speed, mixing until well combined.

3. In a large bowl, whisk together the melted butter, oil, eggs, buttermilk, sour cream, vanilla paste, vinegar and super red gel coloring.

4. With the mixer on low speed, pour the wet ingredients into the bowl of your stand mixer in a slow and steady stream. Mix until just barely incorporated, scraping down the sides of the bowl when necessary. Increase the mixer speed to medium and beat until creamy, no longer than 1 to 2 minutes.

5. Divide the cake batter equally among the prepared pans. Bake for 30 to 35 minutes, or until a toothpick inserted into the center of a cake comes out clean and the cake has pulled away from the edges slightly. Remove from the oven and allow the cakes to cool in their pans for approximately 15 minutes before inverting onto wire racks or a clean countertop. Allow the layers to cool completely before filling and decorating.

TIPS

- Before starting, be sure all your ingredients are at room temperature. This will ensure that all the ingredients will blend and emulsify correctly and will result in a light and fluffy cake.

- This recipe can easily be used for baking cupcakes. Pour the prepared batter into a cupcake tray (or trays) and bake for 18 to 21 minutes, or until a toothpick inserted in the center of one comes out clean. Makes about 48 cupcakes.

FLUFFY LEMON CAKE

MAKES FOUR 6-INCH (15-CM) OR THREE 8-INCH (20-CM) ROUND CAKE LAYERS

This recipe is light and fluffy with a tender crumb and tangy notes of citrus—perfect for a warm summer's day. It is especially refreshing paired with Cream Cheese Frosting (page 164) and Blueberry Filling (page 167).

Vegetable oil spray, for pans

3 cups (375 g) all-purpose flour, plus more for dusting

3 cups (600 g) sugar

2 tsp (9 g) baking powder

¾ tsp salt

3 tbsp (18 g) King Arthur cake enhancer (optional)

1 cup (226 g) unsalted butter, at room temperature

3 large eggs, at room temperature

2 large egg whites, at room temperature

1 cup (240 ml) buttermilk, at room temperature

3 tbsp (45 ml) sour cream, at room temperature

1 tbsp (15 ml) vanilla paste or pure vanilla extract

⅓ cup (80 ml) freshly squeezed and strained lemon juice (from approximately 1 lemon)

⅓ cup (40 g) grated lemon zest (from approximately 2 lemons)

1. Preheat the oven to 350°F (176°C). Grease with vegetable oil spray, dust with flour and line four 6-inch (15-cm) or three 8-inch (20-cm) round cake pans with parchment paper, according to the directions on page 12.

2. Sift the flour, sugar, baking powder, salt and cake enhancer, if using, into the bowl of your stand mixer fitted with the paddle attachment. Set the mixer to the lowest speed, mixing until well combined.

3. With the mixer still running on low speed, slowly add the butter to the bowl. Mix until fine crumbs have formed and no large clumps of butter remain.

4. In a medium-sized bowl, whisk together the eggs, egg whites, buttermilk, sour cream, vanilla, lemon juice and lemon zest.

5. With the mixer on low speed, pour the wet ingredients into the bowl of your stand mixer in a slow and steady stream. Mix until just barely incorporated, scraping down the sides of the bowl when necessary. Increase the mixer speed to medium and beat until creamy, no longer than 1 to 2 minutes.

6. Divide the cake batter equally among the prepared pans. Bake for 30 to 35 minutes, or until a toothpick inserted into the center of a cake comes out clean and the cake has pulled away from the edges slightly. Remove from the oven and allow the cakes to cool in their pans for approximately 15 minutes before inverting onto wire racks or a clean countertop. Allow the layers to cool completely before filling and decorating.

TIPS

- Before starting, be sure all your ingredients are at room temperature. This will ensure that all the ingredients will blend and emulsify correctly and will result in a light and fluffy cake.

- This recipe can easily be used for baking cupcakes. Pour the prepared batter into a cupcake tray (or trays) and bake for 18 to 21 minutes, or until a toothpick inserted in the center of one comes out clean. Makes about 48 cupcakes.

PUMPKIN SPICE CAKE

MAKES FOUR 6-INCH (15-CM) OR THREE 8-INCH (20-CM) ROUND CAKE LAYERS

Pumpkin spice cake is the perfect spicy treat to warm you up in the fall, but it can be enjoyed anytime of the year. Paired with Dulce de Leche (page 176), Fudgy Chocolate Buttercream (page 148) or Cream Cheese Frosting (page 164), this moist and fluffy cake never disappoints.

Vegetable oil spray, for pans

3 cups (375 g) all-purpose flour, plus more for dusting

1 cup (240 ml) vegetable oil

1½ cups (338 g) dark brown sugar

1 cup (200 g) granulated sugar

4 large eggs, at room temperature

¼ cup (60 ml) sour cream, at room temperature

2½ cups (613 g) canned pure pumpkin puree

1 tbsp (15 ml) vanilla paste or pure vanilla extract

2½ tsp (11 g) baking powder

1½ tsp (7 g) baking soda

1½ tsp (6 g) pumpkin pie spice

2 tsp (5 g) ground cinnamon

1 tsp sea salt

1. Preheat the oven to 350°F (176°C). Grease with vegetable oil spray, dust with flour and line four 6-inch (15-cm) or three 8-inch (20-cm) round cake pans with parchment paper, according to the directions on page 12.

2. In a large bowl, whisk together the oil, brown and granulated sugars, eggs, sour cream, pumpkin puree and vanilla until well combined, then set aside.

3. Sift together the flour, baking powder, baking soda, pumpkin pie spice, ground cinnamon and salt into the bowl of your stand mixer that has been fitted with the paddle attachment.

4. Set your mixer to a low speed and slowly pour in the pumpkin mixture. Increase the mixer speed to medium and beat until smooth, no longer than 1 minute. Be sure not to overbeat the batter, as it may cause the cakes to deflate while baking.

5. Divide the cake batter equally among the prepared pans. Bake for 30 to 35 minutes, or until a toothpick inserted into the center of a cake comes out clean and the cake has pulled away from the edges slightly. Remove from the oven and allow the cakes to cool in their pans for approximately 15 minutes before inverting onto wire racks or a clean countertop. Allow the layers to cool completely before filling and decorating.

TIPS

- Before starting, be sure all your ingredients are at room temperature. This will ensure that all the ingredients will blend and emulsify correctly and will result in a light and fluffy cake.

- This recipe can easily be used for baking cupcakes. Pour the prepared batter into a cupcake tray (or trays) and bake for 18 to 21 minutes, or until a toothpick inserted in the center of one comes out clean. Makes about 48 cupcakes.

FUDGY CHOCOLATE BUTTERCREAM

MAKES APPROXIMATELY 8 CUPS (2.4 KG)

Everyone needs a good chocolate buttercream recipe, and this one is perfect for every chocoholic! It is well balanced, creamy and is amazing paired with my Decadent Chocolate Cake recipe (page 139)!

1½ cups (150 g) unsweetened cocoa powder

2 lb (907 g) powdered sugar

Pinch of salt

2 cups (453 g) unsalted butter, at room temperature

1 cup (150 g) milk or dark chocolate chips

1 cup (240 ml) heavy cream

1 tbsp (15 ml) vanilla paste or pure vanilla extract

1. Sift the cocoa powder, powdered sugar and salt into a large bowl and set aside.

2. In the bowl of your stand mixer fitted with the paddle attachment, beat the butter on high speed for 5 minutes, or until pale and increased in volume.

3. While the butter is whipping, place the chocolate in a microwave-safe bowl and microwave for 30-second intervals, stirring in between, until completely melted. Set aside to cool to room temperature.

4. Once the butter has become pale and fluffy and has increased in volume, set the speed to low and add the heavy cream, melted chocolate and vanilla—one at a time—allowing each ingredient to fully incorporate before adding the next.

5. Set the mixer to low speed and begin adding the cocoa mixture, 1 cup (115 g) at a time, until all has been added. Increase the speed to medium and mix until creamy and well incorporated, no longer than 1 to 2 minutes, or excess air bubbles will form in your buttercream.

6. Allow your mixer to run at the lowest setting for about 5 minutes to eliminate any excess air bubbles. Remove any remaining air bubbles by pressing the buttercream against the side of the bowl. You should hear a popping sound as the bubbles come to the surface. Continue to scrape and fold until the buttercream is very smooth and no visible bubbles remain. This can take quite a while sometimes, depending on how much air was incorporated into the buttercream when whipping. Take your time, and don't be afraid to take a breather if your arm is falling off from beating!

This buttercream can be stored for up to 1 week in the refrigerator, or 1 month in the freezer.

GLOSSY VANILLA BUTTER-CREAM

MAKES APPROXIMATELY 8 CUPS (2.4 KG)

This is the perfect marriage between American buttercream and Italian meringue buttercream. I always reach for this recipe when short on time, or when I just need something a little more decadent than American buttercream. It is much quicker and easier to make than traditional Italian meringue buttercream but tastes just as good. This recipe uses pasteurized egg whites and powdered sugar, so there is no cooking or extra equipment required to make it.

2 tbsp (30 ml) fresh lemon juice, plus more for cleaning equipment

2 lb (907 g) powdered sugar

1 cup (240 ml) pasteurized egg whites, at room temperature from the carton

1 tbsp (15 ml) pure vanilla extract (or clear vanilla extract if white buttercream is desired)

Pinch of salt

3 cups (680 g) unsalted butter, at room temperature

1. Wipe down your equipment with lemon juice to eliminate any grease. In the bowl of your stand mixer fitted with the whisk attachment, combine the powdered sugar and the egg whites. Be sure the egg whites are at room temperature to ensure they whip into a meringue.

2. Set the mixer to low speed and mix until the eggs and powdered sugar have turned into a smooth paste. Increase the speed to high and whip until medium peaks form. See page 154.

3. Switch out the whisk attachment for the beater attachment; this will prevent excess air from being incorporated into the buttercream.

4. Set the mixer to medium-low speed and add the vanilla, lemon juice and salt.

5. One spoonful at a time, add the butter and continue to whip until smooth and creamy. It will appear to be curdled at first, but allow it to continue to mix until it has fully come together.

6. Set your mixer to run at the lowest speed for about 5 minutes to eliminate any excess air bubbles. Remove any remaining air bubbles by pressing the buttercream against the side of the bowl with a rubber spatula. You should hear popping sounds as the bubbles come to the surface. Continue to scrape and fold until the buttercream is very smooth and no visible bubbles remain. This can take quite a while sometimes, depending on how much air was incorporated into the buttercream when whipping. Take your time, and don't be afraid to take a breather if your arm is falling off from beating!

TIPS

- Refer to the tips for Italian Meringue Buttercream on page 156 for troubleshooting and best practices for preparing and application.

- This buttercream can be stored for up to 1 week in the refrigerator, or 1 month in the freezer.

ITALIAN MERINGUE BUTTER-CREAM

MAKES 6 TO 7 CUPS (1.8 TO 2.1 KG)

This is my all-time favorite meringue-based buttercream. "Italian" refers to the method of making the meringue (whipping egg whites and hot sugar syrup together) and adding butter to make it into buttercream. There are many ways of making meringue, but this is the most foolproof and mess-free method. This buttercream is smooth, decadent, mousse-like in texture and much less sweet than its American counterpart. It also creates a very shiny finish when piped or smoothed.

Lemon juice, for cleaning equipment

6 large egg whites, at room temperature

1½ cups (300 g) sugar

⅓ cup (80 ml) water

3 cups (680 g) unsalted butter, at room temperature

1 tbsp (15 ml) pure vanilla extract (or clear vanilla if a pure white buttercream is desired)

Pinch of salt

TOOLS

Infrared thermometer

1. Before starting, wipe down all your equipment with lemon juice to eliminate any grease. Place the egg whites in the bowl of your stand mixer fitted with the whisk attachment.

2. In a medium-sized saucepan, combine the sugar and water and place over medium heat. Keep a very close eye on the sugar syrup, as it can boil over and burn easily. Use a thermometer to check the temperature.

3. Once the sugar syrup reaches 230°F (110°C), simultaneously begin whipping the egg whites on a low to medium speed. The egg whites will need to be foamy and frothy by the time the syrup reaches 244°F (118°C). If the egg whites reach this stage before the syrup has reached 244°F (118°C), lower the mixer speed to the lowest setting until this temperature has been reached.

4. When the sugar syrup has reached 244°F (118°C) and the egg whites are frothy, slowly pour the syrup into the mixer bowl in a steady stream at medium-high speed. Allow the meringue to beat on high speed until stiff, glossy peaks have formed and the meringue has cooled significantly—stiff peaks will stand straight upward on the whisk when pulled out of the bowl (see page 154).

5. Switch out the whisk for the beater attachment before continuing; this will prevent excess air being incorporated into the buttercream. Lower the mixer speed to medium and begin to add the butter, one spoonful at a time. Once all the butter has been added, whip on high speed for 2 to 5 minutes, or until fully incorporated. The buttercream may look slightly curdled before it comes together, but do not worry! Continue to whip on high speed until it has become creamy and has turned very glossy.

6. Lower your mixer speed to low and add the vanilla and salt. Allow the buttercream to mix at low speed for about 5 minutes to eliminate any excess air bubbles.

7. Remove any remaining air bubbles by pressing the buttercream against the side of the bowl with a rubber spatula. You should hear popping sounds as the bubbles come to the surface. Continue to scrape and fold until the buttercream is very smooth and no visible bubbles remain. This can take quite a while sometimes, depending on how much air was incorporated into the buttercream when whipping. Take your time, and don't be afraid to take a breather if your arm is falling off from beating!

This buttercream can be stored for up to 1 week in the refrigerator, or 1 month in the freezer. Remove it from the fridge 2 to 3 hours before using and rewhip on low until it has returned to its original consistency after chilling or freezing.

(CONTINUED)

MERINGUE STAGES

Monitor meringue closely while beating and watch for these visual cues. Remember, only a small amount of meringue is needed on the whisk to test the stages.

1. Foamy

When the whisk is raised out of the bowl, the egg whites fall off and are white and foamy. They do not hold any discernible shape. This is the ideal stage to add sugar syrup when making Italian Meringue Buttercream.

2. Soft/Medium Peaks

The meringue will stick to the whisk and has turned quite glossy. It will form a curved peak when it is pulled out of the mixer bowl. This is the ideal stage to begin adding the butter when making Glossy Vanilla Buttercream (page 151).

3. Stiff Peaks

The meringue is very thick and glossy and stands straight upright when the whisk is pulled out of the bowl. This is the ideal stage to add butter when making Italian Meringue Buttercream.

4. Overbeaten

The egg whites were beaten for too long before adding the syrup and have become grainy and separated. To return egg whites back to silky peaks, add 1 to 2 additional egg whites while mixing on medium-low speed. Sometimes a little extra egg white can fix an overbeaten batch.

FLAVOR VARIATIONS

Almond Buttercream

Prepare the Italian Meringue Buttercream, replacing 1 teaspoon of the vanilla extract with 1 teaspoon of almond extract.

Pomegranate Buttercream

Prepare the Italian Meringue Buttercream, replacing 1 teaspoon of the vanilla extract with 1 teaspoon of Get Suckered pomegranate flavoring. Fold in ¼ cup (56 g) of crushed and drained pomegranate arils.

Chocolate-Hazelnut Buttercream

Prepare the Italian Meringue Buttercream, replacing 1 teaspoon of the vanilla extract with 1 teaspoon of Get Suckered hazelnut flavoring. Fold in ¼ cup (75 g) of chocolate-hazelnut spread, such as Nutella.

Pistachio Buttercream

Prepare the Italian Meringue Buttercream, replacing 1 teaspoon of the vanilla extract with 1 teaspoon of Get Suckered pistachio flavoring. Fold in 1 cup (124 g) of finely chopped pistachios.

Strawberry Buttercream

Prepare the Italian Meringue Buttercream, replacing 1 teaspoon of the vanilla extract with 1 teaspoon of Get Suckered strawberry flavoring. Fold in 1 cup (20 g) of powdered freeze-dried strawberries.

(CONTINUED)

ITALIAN MERINGUE BUTTERCREAM (CONTINUED)

TIPS

- If the buttercream looks soupy, it is most likely because the butter and/or the meringue is too warm. Place the bowl into the fridge for 10 to 15 minutes and rewhip. Alternatively, you can place ice packs around the base of the mixer bowl to cool the meringue as it whips.

- If the buttercream separates and looks grainy, it is most likely because the butter was too cold when it was added to the meringue. Place the mixer bowl on top of a double boiler and heat until about one-quarter of the buttercream has melted (mainly around the edges of the bowl). Rewhip the buttercream until it is creamy and has come back together.

- If your buttercream has sugar granules in it after making, it is most likely because the sugar syrup did not reach the correct temperature. Using an infrared thermometer is advised as it is far more accurate than a regular candy thermometer.

- If your meringue failed to whip up to begin with, it may be due to not cleaning your equipment properly. Any small amount of egg yolk getting in the meringue will prevent it from whipping up as it is a fat. Be sure to wipe everything thoroughly to eliminate any grease in your bowl, whisk or spoons. Wash your hands well before starting to make sure any excess oils are not present when handling the eggs.

- Coloring a meringue-based buttercream is slightly different from coloring American buttercream. You can use either an oil-based colorant or the following method: Place one-third of the buttercream you are coloring in a microwave-safe container, then microwave for 10-second intervals until completely melted. Add the gel coloring and stir until well incorporated. Add the melted buttercream back to the bowl of uncolored buttercream and stir to incorporate. Melting helps the color blend into the buttercream far more easily than if you were to add the coloring directly to it without melting.

MIDNIGHT BLACK BUTTER-CREAM

MAKES 6 TO 7 CUPS (1.8 TO 2.1 KG)

This is my go-to black buttercream recipe, which has been tried and loved by many! It has a unique ingredient called black cocoa to achieve its dark color naturally. The cocoa tastes just like an Oreo, as it is in fact the same cocoa used to make the famous cookies! Combined with the sugar, the bitterness from the cocoa is perfectly balanced to create a uniquely flavored and incredibly delicious buttercream!

1½ cups (232 g) Dutch-processed black cocoa powder (I prefer The Cocoa Trader brand)

2 lb (907 g) powdered sugar

2 cups (452 g) unsalted butter, at room temperature

1 cup (240 ml) heavy cream

1 tbsp (15 ml) vanilla paste or pure vanilla extract

Pinch of salt

Wilton black gel coloring (depending on how dark your black cocoa is; optional)

1. Sift the black cocoa and powdered sugar into a large bowl and set aside.

2. In the bowl of your stand mixer fitted with the paddle attachment, beat the butter on high speed for 5 minutes, or until pale and increased in volume.

3. Once the butter has become fluffy and has increased in volume, lower the speed to low and add the heavy cream, vanilla and salt.

4. With the mixer still running at low speed, begin to add the cocoa mixture, 1 cup (135 g) at a time, until all has been added. Increase the speed to medium and mix until creamy and well incorporated, no longer than 1 to 2 minutes, or excess air bubbles will form in your buttercream.

5. If needed, add the black gel coloring at this point. Allow your mixer to run at the lowest setting for about 5 minutes to eliminate any excess air bubbles. Remove any remaining air bubbles by pressing the buttercream against the side of the bowl. You should hear popping sounds as the bubbles come to the surface and burst. Continue to scrape and fold until the buttercream is very smooth and no visible bubbles remain. This can take quite a while sometimes, depending on how much air was incorporated into the buttercream when whipping. Take your time, and don't be afraid to take a breather if your arm is falling off from beating!

This buttercream can be stored for up to 1 week in the refrigerator, or 1 month in the freezer.

TIP

- Different brands of black cocoa create different shades and some are much darker than others. To achieve a true black, I recommend using The Cocoa Trader brand black cocoa.

MIDNIGHT BLACK BUTTER-CREAM— METHOD 2

MAKES 6 TO 7 CUPS (1.8 TO 2.1 KG)

This method uses regular unsweetened cocoa in place of black cocoa, which tastes more like dark chocolate rather than an Oreo cookie. This variation is perfect for any recipe that requires a chocolate flavor profile and is a simple way to make black buttercream when you do not have black cocoa on hand.

1½ cups (167 g) unsweetend cocoa powder

2 lb (907 g) powdered sugar

2 cups (452 g) unsalted butter, at room temperature

1 cup (240 ml) heavy cream

1 tbsp (15 ml) vanilla paste or pure vanilla extract

Pinch of salt

Wilton black gel coloring

1. Follow steps 1–4 of the Midnight Black Buttercream recipe on page 157, omitting the black cocoa powder and substituting it with the unsweetened cocoa powder.

2. Add 1 to 2 teaspoons (5 to 10 ml) of black gel coloring, if desired, and mix on low speed for 2 minutes until the color is well incorporated. Your buttercream will not be black in color at this point, but only a dark gray. Cover and allow the buttercream to mature in color overnight either at room temperature or in the refrigerator. Dark hues, such as blue and black, need time to mature their colors. After 24 hours, your buttercream should be pitch black! The longer you allow it to mature, the darker it will be. Because this method uses some gel coloring, there will be a little staining, but far less than if you were to start with a vanilla buttercream.

TIP

- I would not advise using a vanilla buttercream and adding gel coloring to achieve black. An entire bottle of black gel coloring will be needed and will probably only result in a dark gray color. Excess amounts of gel coloring will stain your mouth as well as give your buttercream a bitter aftertaste.

OTHER WAYS TO COLOR YOUR BUTTERCREAM

Roxy & Rich Midnight Black powdered coloring

There will still be some staining, but considerably less than straight gel coloring. Be sure to mix the powder into ½ to 1 teaspoon of water before adding to your buttercream.

Sweet Sticks Edible Art Decorative Cake Paint (black)

Once chilled, a cake frosted with Simple Vanilla Buttercream (page 18) can be painted black using paints, such as Sweet Sticks edible paints. Keep in mind that the paint may create a different texture, flavor or finish on your buttercream. These paints can only be used on American buttercream.

Ganache

Instead of using buttercream, you could consider trying dark Chocolate Ganache Frosting (page 163) tinted black. The amount of gel coloring needed will depend on how dark your chocolate is. Add more gel coloring when using milk chocolate and less when using dark chocolate.

WHITE CHOCOLATE GANACHE FROSTING

MAKES APPROXIMATELY 4 CUPS (1.1 KG)

Ganache drips are amazing, but have you ever tried using ganache as a filling, or to frost an entire cake? Ganache can be used in place of buttercream in almost any situation, is very versatile and holds up well in warm climates. It sets quite firmly, which makes it an amazing base to paint onto, but can also be whipped to create a fluffy frosting.

24 oz (680 g) white chocolate chips (I prefer Ghirardelli brand)

1 cup (240 ml) heavy cream

2 tsp (10 ml) Wilton whitener gel

1. In a microwave-safe container, combine the white chocolate and heavy cream, and microwave for 30-second intervals, gently stirring in between, until completely melted.

2. Once completely melted, add the whitener gel and gently stir until the color has been well incorporated.

3. Cover and chill in the fridge overnight, or until set. The ganache will thicken as it sits. Reheat in the microwave for 30 seconds after refrigerating to bring it back to a frosting consistency. Stir until smooth before using.

CHOCOLATE GANACHE FROSTING

MAKES APPROXIMATELY 4 CUPS (1.1 KG)

This frosting has a beautiful gloss when applied, and has a decadent truffle-like flavor and consistency. Chocolate Ganache Frosting is a great option when stacking cakes as it does not melt as easily as buttercream and sets firmly.

24 oz (680 g) milk or dark chocolate chips (I prefer Ghirardelli brand)

2 cups (480 ml) heavy cream

1. In a microwave-safe container, combine the chocolate and heavy cream, and microwave for 30-second intervals, gently stirring in between, until completely melted.

2. Cover and chill in the fridge overnight, or until set. The ganache will thicken as it sits. Microwave for 30 seconds after refrigerating to bring it back to a frosting consistency. Stir until smooth before using.

CREAM CHEESE FROSTING

MAKES 6 TO 7 CUPS (900 G TO 1 KG)

This frosting is thicker than the average cream cheese frosting to ensure it is stable enough to pipe and hold its shape while decorating. The cream cheese flavor may be more subtle than other recipes but can be increased by adding extra flavoring without affecting the stability at all.

1 cup (226 g) unsalted butter, at room temperature

1 cup (230 g) cream cheese, cold

1 tbsp (15 ml) pure vanilla extract (or clear vanilla extract if white frosting is desired)

1 tsp Get Suckered Cream Cheese flavoring (optional)

Pinch of salt

2 tsp (10 ml) fresh lemon juice

2 lb (907 g) powdered sugar

1. In the bowl of your stand mixer fitted with the beater attachment, beat together the butter and cream cheese on high speed for 5 minutes, or until very pale and increased in volume.

2. Turn the mixer to the lowest setting and add the vanilla, cream cheese flavoring, if using, salt and lemon juice to reduce sweetness.

3. Begin adding the powdered sugar, 1 cup (120 g) at a time, until all has been added. Beat at a medium speed until the buttercream is smooth and creamy, no longer than 1 to 2 minutes, or excess air bubbles will form.

4. Set your mixer to run at the lowest speed for about 5 minutes to eliminate any excess bubbles. Remove any remaining air bubbles by pressing the buttercream against the side of the bowl with a rubber spatula. You should hear a popping sound as the bubbles come to the surface and burst. Continue to scrape and fold until the buttercream is very smooth and no visible bubbles remain. This can take quite a while sometimes, depending on how much air was incorporated into the buttercream when whipping. Take your time, and don't be afraid to take a breather if your arm is falling off from beating!

This buttercream can be stored for up to 1 week in the refrigerator, or 1 month in the freezer.

BERRY FILLING

MAKES APPROXIMATELY 1 CUP (335 G)

A berry-filled cake is perfect for any occasion. It adds moisture, natural sweetness and a lot of flavor to a cake—and is especially delicious when paired with a light buttercream, such as Italian meringue. Any type of berries can be used for this recipe. Try blueberries, strawberries, raspberries, blackberries and even a combination of all of them! If it's the middle of winter you can use frozen berries in place of fresh. This filling can be made in the summertime and frozen to use later in the year when fresh fruit is not as readily available. Besides using it as a filling for cakes, try drizzling it on top of ice cream, waffles, cheesecake and even pies!

2 cups (290 g) fresh or (310 g) frozen berries (if using frozen, bring to room temperature and drain excess juice)

3 tbsp (45 ml) water

¾ cup (150 g) sugar

3 tbsp (25 g) cornstarch

2 tsp (10 ml) fresh lemon juice

1. Place the berries in a blender, reserving 1 to 2 tablespoons (10 to 20 g) of whole berries to add later, if desired. Add the water to the blender and pulse until completely smooth.

2. In a small saucepan, combine the sugar and cornstarch and place over medium heat.

3. Add the berry puree and lemon juice to the pan, stirring to combine. Stir constantly until the mixture has thickened significantly. Be sure to watch carefully to prevent the berry mixture from burning on the bottom of the pan.

4. Once the berry mixture has thickened and coats the back of a spoon without running off, it is ready. If you used berries that naturally contain a lot of seeds (e.g., raspberries) you may want to run the mixture through a sieve for a less crunchy texture. Save 1 teaspoon of the seeds to add later if you like a little bit of crunch.

5. If desired, stir in the reserved whole berries and/or retained seeds to add some extra texture to your filling.

Allow to cool for 15 minutes and transfer to an airtight container. Store in the refrigerator for up to 1 week, or in the freezer for up to 3 months.

TIPS

- If using such berries as strawberries, you may not need to add water to the recipe, as they are naturally very juicy already.

- Strain the berries well before using to prevent a runny filling.

CHERRY FILLING

MAKES APPROXIMATELY 1½ CUPS (400 G)

Cherry season is always a favorite in my household and is looked forward to all year long! Cherry filling is so quick and easy to whip up and makes a delicious filling for cakes, pies and even ice cream!

¾ cup (150 g) sugar

2 tbsp (16 g) cornstarch

2 cups (310 g) pitted fresh or frozen cherries, drained

2 tbsp (30 ml) fresh lemon juice

2 tbsp (30 ml) water

¼ tsp almond extract (optional)

1. In a small saucepan, combine the sugar and cornstarch.

2. Add the cherries, lemon juice and water and place over medium heat.

3. Bring to a slow simmer, stirring continuously to prevent the mixture from burning. Lower the heat to low and allow it to simmer for about 10 minutes, stirring occasionally.

4. Once thickened, remove from the heat and add the almond extract, if desired.

Let cool for 15 minutes before transferring to an airtight container. Store in the refrigerator for up to 1 week, or in the freezer for up to 3 months.

APPLE FILLING

MAKES APPROXIMATELY 1½ CUPS (400 G)

This filling is made of crisp green apples with a hint of spice for a delicious addition to any dessert. Apple filling is simple to make and can even be used to fill homemade pies or tarts.

½ cup (115 g) dark brown sugar

3 tbsp (25 g) cornstarch

2 medium-sized Granny Smith apples, cored, peeled and diced

2 tbsp (28 g) unsalted butter

1 tbsp (15 ml) fresh lemon juice

1 tsp ground cinnamon

¼ tsp apple pie spice

1½ cups (360 ml) water

1. In a small saucepan, combine the brown sugar and cornstarch.

2. Add the diced apples, butter, lemon juice, cinnamon, apple pie spice and water and place over medium heat.

3. Bring to a slow simmer, stirring constantly to prevent the mixture from burning. Set the heat to low and allow it to simmer until thickened and softened, stirring occasionally.

Once thickened and cooled for 15 minutes, transfer to an airtight container. Store in the refrigerator for up to 1 week, or in the freezer for up to 3 months.

LEMON CURD

MAKES APPROXIMATELY 1½ CUPS (375 G)

Lemon curd is a uniquely tangy filling for cakes and lots of other desserts. It can even be eaten on toast for a tasty breakfast treat! This filling balances out the sweetness of the buttercream and just melts in your mouth!

5 large egg yolks (see Tip)

2 large eggs

Zest of 2 lemons

½ cup (120 ml) fresh lemon juice

2 cups (400 g) sugar

½ cup (113 g) unsalted butter, cold and cubed

1. In the top of a double boiler, or in a heatproof bowl, combine the egg yolks and eggs.

2. Add the lemon zest and juice as well as the sugar to the egg mixture.

3. Place the double boiler top or bowl atop a pot of water that is simmering over medium heat. Be sure the water is not touching the bottom of the upper vessel.

4. Whisk the egg mixture constantly to prevent it from burning on the bottom. The curd will slowly thicken and begin sticking to the sides of the pan. This can sometimes take a while, so have patience and allow it to thicken slowly. If cooked too quickly, you risk scrambling the eggs, which is what we are trying to avoid by heating it slowly. Once the curd coats the back of a spoon without running off, it can be removed from the heat.

5. Place the cold cubes of butter in the thickened curd, stirring until completely melted. The cold butter helps the curd stop cooking and cools it down significantly.

6. Run the curd through a fine-mesh sieve to remove any lumps. Allow the curd to set and chill completely before using to fill a cake.

Let cool for 15 minutes before transferring to an airtight container. Refrigerate up to 1 week, or in the freezer for up to 3 months.

TIP

- You can always save the whites to use for Italian Meringue Buttercream (page 152) or another dessert later.

LIME CURD

MAKES APPROXIMATELY 1½ CUPS (375 G)

Lime curd has a sweet yet tangy flavor and an ultra creamy consistency. It's perfect for summer-themed cakes.

5 large egg yolks (see Tip)

2 large eggs

Zest of 2 limes

½ cup (120 ml) fresh lime juice

2 cups (400 g) sugar

½ cup (113 g) unsalted butter, cold and cubed

1. You can very easily make Lime Curd instead of Lemon Curd by switching out a few ingredients! Follow the steps for Lemon Curd, replacing the lemon juice and zest with equal quantities of lime juice and zest.

Let cool for 15 minutes before transferring to an airtight container. Refrigerate up to 1 week, or in the freezer for up to 3 months.

CHEESE-CAKE FILLING

MAKES APPROXIMATELY 1½ CUPS (355 G)

Cheesecake is such a classic and makes a perfectly creamy filling for cakes and desserts alike. The best part about this filling is that it's a no-bake recipe! Try adding it as a filling to cupcakes, turn it into a no-bake cheesecake or simply eat it straight off the spoon—it's that good!

1 cup (225 g) cream cheese, chilled

½ cup (60 g) powdered sugar

¼ cup (60 ml) heavy cream

1 tsp vanilla

1. In a large bowl, combine the cream cheese and powdered sugar. Beat on high speed with a handheld mixer until smooth and creamy.

2. Add the heavy cream and vanilla. Continue to mix until well combined, 2 to 3 minutes.

Transfer any unused filling to an airtight container and store in the refrigerator for up to 1 week.

DULCE DE LECHE

MAKES APPROXIMATELY 1 CUP (396 G)

Dulce de leche, translated from Spanish, means "candy made of milk." This is a thick, rich caramel made by boiling condensed milk for an extended amount of time. Growing up, my mum would fill all our birthday cakes with dulce de leche, and it soon became a much-loved tradition in my baking as well. You can sometimes find premade cans in the Latin section of your grocery store, but it is just as easy to make at home.

1 unopened (14-oz [396-g]) can sweetened condensed milk

1. Place the unopened can of sweetened condensed milk on its side in a large pot. Fill the pot with water, making sure the water covers the can by at least 2 inches (5 cm).

2. Set the pot over medium-high heat and bring to a boil.

3. Reduce the heat to medium-low and allow the pot to simmer steadily for about 3 hours. Be sure to check on the pot from time to time to see whether more water needs to be added so as to keep the can covered at all times.

4. After 3 hours, remove the pot from the heat. Allow the water in the pot to stop boiling, then using metal tongs, remove the can from the pot. Transfer to a wire rack to cool completely. Once completely cool to the touch (be very careful to allow the can to cool before opening, as the heat can cause pressurization), open the can as normal and transfer the cooked caramel to an airtight container.

Dulce de Leche can be stored in an airtight container in the refrigerator for up to 3 weeks.

TIP

- The amount of time stated in the directions is ideal for creating a rich, thick, amber-colored caramel—the perfect thickness for filling or coating cakes. Boiling the can for shorter amounts of time will result in a thinner and lighter caramel for drizzling, so feel free to experiment with the amount of time you boil the can to find your preferred flavor and texture.

EDIBLE COOKIE DOUGH

MAKES APPROXIMATELY 2 CUPS (600 G)

Ever felt tempted to snack on that chocolate chip cookie dough while making cookies? Now, you can indulge without being afraid of getting a tummy ache. This cookie dough is made without any eggs and uses heat-treated flour, making it a delicious and indulgent snack any day of the week! Try adding it between cake layers or rolling it into balls for a cute decoration.

2 cups (250 g) all-purpose flour

1 cup (226 g) unsalted butter, at room temperature

2 tbsp (30 ml) vanilla paste or pure vanilla extract

1 cup (225 g) packed dark brown sugar

2 tbsp (30 ml) heavy cream

1 tsp sea salt

1 cup (170 g) milk or dark chocolate chips

1. Preheat the oven to 350°F (176°C). Line a baking sheet with parchment paper.

2. Spread the flour on the prepared baking sheet. Bake until the flour reaches 160°F (70°C). You can check the temperature, using an infrared thermometer, but it should take 5 to 10 minutes. The flour is now heat treated and is completely safe to eat. Set aside until cool.

3. In a medium-sized bowl or the bowl of your stand mixer fitted with the beater attachment, combine the butter, vanilla paste, brown sugar and heavy cream. Beat until smooth and creamy.

4. Fold in the flour, sea salt and chocolate chips. Wrap and refrigerate for approximately 10 minutes, or until the dough is no longer sticky.

Store any unused cookie dough in an airtight container in the refrigerator for up to 5 days.

SUGAR COOKIES

MAKES 25 TO 30 MEDIUM-SIZED COOKIES

These vanilla sugar cookies are the perfect balance of sweet and salty, with a soft and chewy texture. Get creative with your cookie cutters; this recipe was created to hold its shape while baking, so don't worry about your beautiful cutouts spreading in the oven.

3 cups (375 g) all-purpose flour, plus more for dusting

1 tsp baking powder

½ tsp salt

1 cup (226 g) unsalted butter, at room temperature

1 cup (200 g) sugar

1 tbsp (15 ml) pure vanilla extract

2 large eggs

1. In a large bowl, whisk together the flour, baking powder and salt, then set aside.

2. In the bowl of your stand mixer fitted with the paddle attachment, beat together the butter and sugar until smooth and creamy, about 2 minutes.

3. Add the vanilla to the butter mixture and beat well for another minute. Don't forget to scrape down the sides of the bowl as you go. Set your mixer speed to low and add the eggs. With the mixer still running on low speed, add the flour mixture, 1 cup (125 g) at a time. Mix until just incorporated and the dough has formed a ball around the paddle.

4. Wrap the ball of dough in plastic wrap, then press into a disk shape approximately 1 inch (2.5 cm) in thickness. Place the dough in the refrigerator and chill for 30 minutes.

5. Preheat the oven to 350°F (176°C). Remove the chilled dough from the refrigerator and place on a floured surface. Roll out to approximately ¼ inch (6 mm) in thickness. Cut out the dough with your desired cookie cutters, and place 2 inches (5 cm) apart on an ungreased baking sheet.

6. Bake for 7 to 10 minutes, or until the edges start to look slightly golden in color. Remove from the oven and transfer the baked cookies to a wire rack. Allow to cool completely before decorating.

ROYAL ICING

MAKES ABOUT 2 CUPS (280 G)

This is an easy-peasy cookie icing you can whip up in no time. This icing can be used to decorate fancy cutout cookies and even to create transfer decorations. Royal icing hardens and dries with a shiny finish, which makes it the perfect treat to wrap up and send to a friend.

Lemon juice, for cleaning equipment

4 cups (480 g) powdered sugar

5 tbsp (75 ml) water, at room temperature

¼ cup (36 g) Wilton meringue powder

½ to 1 tsp pure vanilla extract

1. Wipe down your stand mixer bowl and whisk attachment with lemon juice to eliminate any fat. (Grease or fat will prevent a meringue from whipping up.)

2. Place the sugar, water, Wilton meringue powder and vanilla in the bowl of your stand mixer fitted with the whisk attachment, or in a large bowl. Set the mixer to low speed and mix until everything is well combined, then increase the speed to high. Beat until stiff peaks have formed—about 6 minutes with a stand mixer or 10 to 15 minutes with a hand mixer (see page 154 for reference).

3. Cover and let the icing sit for approximately 15 minutes to allow any excess air bubbles to rise to the surface. The icing will be at a stiff consistency at this point.

Store any unused icing in an airtight container in the refrigerator for up to 3 days.

Stiff Consistency

Some decorations require a stiff consistency for piping things like flowers, transfers and outlines. Stiff consistency icing will form a stiff point on the beater when pulled out of the bowl.

Flooding Consistency

Flooding-consistency icing is ideal for filling in the large areas of cookies and is thinner than stiff-consistency icing.

Add 1 teaspoon of water at a time to the stiff icing and stir gently. Scoop up some of the icing onto a spoon—if it sinks back down and becomes invisible within 10 seconds, it has reached flooding consistency.

If you added too much water and the icing has become runny, add 1 tablespoon (5 g) of sifted powdered sugar and test again. Be sure to cover the icing immediately with plastic wrap after preparing.

RESOURCES

SPRINKLES AND EDIBLE GLITTER

There are so many amazing sprinkle suppliers out there, but some of my favorites are from Sprinkle Pop, Fancy Sprinkles, Super Streusel and Sweetapolita. Roxy & Rich has a wide variety of edible glitters, which I use quite often in this book! Most companies ship worldwide, so you should be able to order them no matter where you are in the world. I highly encourage you to buy whatever you can find locally and try mixing blends yourself, too. You have far more control over the colors and themes this way and it is a great place to start. Sprinkle Pop allows you to create your own customized blends, which is such a fun way to personalize your dessert art even further!

GENERAL BAKING SUPPLIES

Michaels is a great place to find everything baking and craft-related and is very affordable. I purchase molds, gel coloring, baking tools, cookie cutters, decor and any other last-minute supplies needed here.

BACKDROPS AND PAPER

Besides all things cakes and dessert, photography and videography are other huge passions of mine! I'm asked all the time how I set up for photographs and am always happy to share behind-the-scenes tips. Some of my favorite backdrops to use for photos are from a company called Ink and Elm, and are made from a sturdy vinyl material. They clean up well after spills and accidents, which makes them ideal for food photography. I also use large paper sheets or rolls for photographs. You can find professional photo backdrop paper from such companies as Savage, but in a pinch, you can find paper sheets at any craft or office supply store.

PROPS/SEASONAL DECOR

One of my favorite stores to shop at for photo props, bakeware, seasonal decor and unique candy is TJ Maxx. It always has a huge assortment of affordable products and is constantly restocking with new and exciting things, so you never know what you're going to find.

CAKE STANDS

Some women own a collection of shoes, but I prefer cake stands! Just like that perfect accessory to an outfit, a cake stand is an extension of the cake itself. The style can either make or break the overall look. I know it may sound dramatic, but it's true. I love finding unique vintage stands at local antique stores, but you can also find them at such places as Amalfi Décor, Etsy, Amazon, TJ Maxx and Pier 1 Imports. My favorites are marble or milk glass plated.

AMAZON

I live in a small town in the middle of nowhere, so Amazon is one of my go-to places for finding cake supplies, decor, tools and just about everything in between. If you're not sure where to find it, Amazon probably has it!

WILTON

Wilton is my preferred brand for all things cake pans, piping tips, piping bags, cupcake liners, decorating spatulas and lots more. Wilton is a well-known company in the United States and is very dependable for high-quality products and seasonal baking supplies.

MIXERS

My stand mixer of choice is KitchenAid brand and is very accessible within the United States. These mixers are so powerful and last for years. The model used in my kitchen the most frequently is the Artisan mixer, but there are many to choose from. The type of baking you plan on doing will determine which model you'll need (e.g., a larger mixer for a home-based baking business). If you do not have access to a stand mixer, I highly recommend purchasing an electric hand mixer to create the recipes within this book.

POWDERED AND GEL COLORING

The most vibrant and highly pigmented gel coloring I have come to love are from Chefmaster, which offers a variety of different colors and products. Another brand worth noting is Americolor, which works well also. In recent months, I have come to love using powdered coloring from such companies as Roxy & Rich, as well as The Sugar Art. Both create beautifully deep shades, which I would recommend using for such colors as red, navy and black in place of gel coloring.

TEMPLATES

To find any of the templates used in this book, visit cakedesignbysheri.com. From there, print out your desired template, trace it onto parchment paper and follow the directions of whichever tutorial you are working through.

ACKNOWLEDGMENTS

To my amazing husband, Zack—for staying up late, taking photos, driving to the store at midnight, caring for tired kids, but most of all for always being there as a true friend and confidant. This book never would have happened without you and your endless amount of patience. You challenge me to be the best version of myself and believe in me even when I don't. I'm so lucky to have you in my life.

To my children, Nathaniel and Acacia. Thank you for constantly bringing all the fun and laughter. You guys are an endless source of energy and inspire me to be a better person every single day. Love you both to the moon and back!

To my mum and dad—thank you for encouraging me in only the way a parent could. I am thankful for a diverse and well-traveled upbringing, and for being taught to always work hard in everything I do. I love you, Mum, and wish Dad could be here.

To Arnold—you have been so patient throughout this entire process and have put up with all our crazy ideas. Thank you for your generosity, encouragement and support. It means the world.

To Issabelle—thank you for being so helpful and answering all my photo-related questions to get this book finished; you are a lifesaver, and I'm so grateful for your insight and knowledge.

To Taryn—thank you for answering my never-ending questions and sharing all your knowledge. You constantly push me to try new things and to continue reinventing and innovating.

To NYcake—for sending me an endless amount of piping bags and other supplies to use when creating this book. I appreciate your love and support so much.

To my editor Franny—thank you for your immense amount of patience and your eye for detail. I couldn't have asked for a kinder and more thoughtful writing partner during this process. You always communicate in the sweetest yet clear manner, which could not have been a better fit for making this project flow smoothly. I'm forever grateful to have been able to trust your direction and to know that you are always in my corner.

To the entire Page Street Publishing team—you are always open to hear my ideas and truly made my book dreams come to life. Thank you for your expertise, knowledge and patience during this process.

To my readers and cake community—none of these opportunities would have been possible without the constant love and support of this amazing community. You all inspire, challenge and encourage me daily, and many of you have become close friends in the process. I hope this book encourages you to access your inner creative soul and gives you the confidence to express it. Happy caking, lovely friends. xx

ABOUT THE AUTHOR

Sheri is an award-winning, self-taught cake artist who started baking cakes to relieve the newfound stresses of motherhood. After everyone had gone to bed, Sheri practiced smoothing cakes and learned how to hold a piping bag from her small home kitchen. Fast-forward a couple of years, Sheri is the face behind the popular baking accounts "Cake Design by Sheri" on YouTube and Instagram. Her distinct visual style, ranging from rich blacks to explosive neons, has been featured by *People*, *CNBC*, POPSUGAR and Yahoo, inspiring baking trends around the globe. Sheri has spent her life traveling the world and has lived in South Africa, New Zealand, Australia and now the United States with her husband and two children.

INDEX